This book comes to you a[...] Trust, as part of our Book[...] Over 150,000 of these bo[...] over Scotland.

Book Week Scotland takes place from 25 November– 1 December 2013 and is Scotland's annual national celebration of books and reading. Throughout the week, libraries, schools, museums, arts venues, charities and workplaces will host a packed programme of events, with ways for people of all ages to celebrate the pleasure of books and reading. Visit **www.bookweekscotland.com** for full listings of Book Week Scotland events, reading inspiration, book lists, podcasts, author interviews, and much more.

Scottish Book Trust is the leading agency for the promotion of literature, reading and writing in Scotland, developing innovative projects to encourage adults and children to read, write and be inspired by books. It is a non-profit organisation funded by Creative Scotland, sponsorship and other grants.

For details of our exciting events programme for Book Week Scotland, more projects by Scottish Book Trust, book recommendations and more, sign up to our newsletter at **http://bit.ly/treasuresbook**.

Treasures

What do we treasure most?

www.scottishbooktrust.com

First published 2013 by Scottish Book Trust, Sandeman House, Trunk's Close, 55 High Street, Edinburgh EH1 1SR

www.scottishbooktrust.com

The authors' right to be identified as an author of this book under the Copyright, Patents and Designs Act 1988 has been asserted.

A CIP catalogue record for this book is available from the British Library

Typeset by 3btype in 10pt Sabon

Printed and bound by CPI Group (UK) Ltd, Croydon, CR0 4YY

Scottish Book Trust makes every effort to ensure that the paper used in this book has been legally sourced from well-managed and certified forests.

Cover design by Anna Patience. Cover illustrations by Esther Kent. Photographs by Chris Scott. The front cover photograph is one of the authors of the stories within this book, and there are 8 editions of the book with different authors shown. The cover models are: Christine Ashworth, Udita Banerjee, Linda Brown, Thomas Clark, Carroll Johnstone, Peter Lomax, Gill Monaghan and Iain Reynolds.

This is a free book, designed to be read alone or in groups, enjoyed, shared and passed on to friends. This book is gifted to you by Scottish Book Trust for Book Week Scotland 2013.

ePub and Kindle editions of this book are available from **www.scottishbooktrust.com/Treasures** or from Amazon

COMHAIRLE NAN LEABHRAICHEAN
THE GAELIC BOOKS COUNCIL

Contents

Wearables

Tools

Recreation

Stories in italics are by established writers.

Recorded memories

Found objects

Jewellery

Wearables

Uncle Moses' Boots

Carole E. and John Barrowman

Tell us the one about the...

We are a family of storytellers. Whenever we gather in one place, there are stories to be told – tales of Uncle Moses who slept in his boots for fear of someone stealing them, of the ghostly terrier who haunted Tollcross park howling 'give me back my bone', of Sandy who died alone at Ypres never knowing he had a son, of Jeannie running a Glasgow factory during the Second World War only to be dismissed when the men returned, of our dad hiding for six hours in a coal bunker just to leap out at the perfect moment to terrify his young bride (our mum).

These tales of love and glory and courage and curiosity; of hardship and mischief (lots of it) have shaped us. Perhaps not surprisingly, then, two of the objects we treasure are an antique lap desk and a silver pocket watch (Carole has the lap desk and John the watch) because they are tangible conduits to our family's past and they tell stories.

Inlaid with triangles of mahogany and maple, the lap desk unfolds in three sections: one with pigeon holes and crannies for storing pens and papers, the second with two inkwells with the pots still intact, and the third opens to a lectern of sorts with a leather writing surface.

Papa Butler (our mum's dad) inherited the desk from his mother, Maggie Martin, who lived in a cottage in Strathaven. The lap desk may have been given to Maggie as a gift from her mother or it may have been her mother's and her mother's before that. We're not sure. Lap desks were fashionable as far back as the 1700s and were sometimes called 'lady's travelling boxes'.

The lap desk was where Maggie kept her recipe for strawberry jam, a jar of which she'd give to our gran, Murn, before they'd get on the train back to Shettleston after a Sunday visit. She'd give her son (our papa) a box of Swan's Vesta matches and her granddaughter (our mum) a 'poke' of peppermints and a 'thrup'nny'.

The lap desk was where Maggie drafted the letter insisting that our gran pack a suitcase for our mum (a child at the time) and get her on the first train out of Glasgow before the German Luftwaffe bombed any more of the Clyde ship yards. Our mum remembers Maggie meeting her at the station in grey and black and wearing stylish ankle boots.

The lap desk was where Maggie wrote the notes thanking friends and neighbours for their kindnesses after her husband, Alexander, died suddenly, leaving her a widow with two sons. And when, decades later, she gave her son, Andrew (our papa) the lap desk, he kept a lifetime of letters and papers in its nooks and crannies. In turn, he passed the desk along to his daughter and she then to hers– a 'lady's travelling box' again.

The silver pocket watch tells a similar tale. Our grandma, Emily Barrowman, bought the pocket watch, its matching chain and small folding knife as a wedding present for her husband, John (Jock to all who loved him). It was 1926 and Jock had left the mines of Scotland to find work in the mills of Steubenville, Ohio. Emily joined him in America, but they never settled.

The silver pocket watch marked Emily and Jock's time in the Ohio River valley where their homesickness and a brother's rheumatic fever eventually brought them home to Scotland.

The silver pocket watch marked Emily's return to the banks of the Ohio River valley decades later when she and her son, John (our dad), remembered those tough early years of a marriage that lasted until death parted them.

The silver pocket watch marked the times Jock's grandson and his namesake, John, wore the watch when he stood in The Hub as Captain Jack on *Torchwood*. The watch was tucked in the pocket of Jack's waistcoat, a real life artefact in a make-believe world and a reminder of the nobility of character that the watch represented.

We never met Maggie. Papa Barrowman died when we were young. The lining in the lap desk is torn and the watch keeps time erratically. But like the faint imprint of letters on the leather of the desk or the small scratches on the watch's face, legacies are etched over time in our hearts and if we're lucky they travel across generations in the ordinary objects we treasure.

The Boots

Heather J.C. Beaton

A favourite possession should change you; enhance your life. It should make you better than you were without it and that is what my walking boots do for me.

Without them I'm just a girl. Just trying to make my way through this world as best I can, but tie on my Meindl walking boots with their soles that glitter from the Glenuig sands and their creases and wrinkles which make them echoes of my feet and suddenly I'm in control. I'm no longer buffeted by ceaseless winds but am newly confident of my true path and way. They protect me – never a blister or a wet toe, no matter how many bogs I walk through, and all the while they make me strong and ambitious. That mountain which was a monster in the sky suddenly becomes a perfectly achievable challenge. With my boots on my feet I am no longer constrained by normal fears and worries but the world instead takes on a brighter and more victorious light. The greens glitter and beg me to walk upon them, the blues vibrate with life and love and happiness and the browns shimmer with energy that is asking to be utilised. 'Climb me', cry the tall trees, and with my boots on, I do.

Only with my boots on am I truly free of my own and modern life's pressures (do this, do that) and that freedom is, perhaps, the most precious possession of all.

Daddy's Bunnet

Marion Jean Bryans

Daddy always wore a bunnet
Before going out his front door
Hands automatically reached for the bunnet,
Folded in his pocket.

Rain, hail or shine,
There it was – atop his head
To the shipyards, the pictures, the ballet,
His bunnet – his smell
Manly, distinct, unique.

When he died I was gutted.
I wore his dressing gown
To feel him touch my skin.
His folded bunnet in a plastic bag.

In the early days of grief
Often I fondled that cap,
Pressed my nose – deep inside, inhaling his fragrance,
Instantly invoking his presence,
Bittersweet tears.

Time moved on,
Squashed on the top shelf of a wardrobe
This forgotten treasure.
Years later, sudden refinding,
A smile delights my face.

Tentatively opening the bag,
Wondering if his essence persists,
A miracle –
The hint of him, as strong as ever fills my senses.
Silence –
Lost in reverie I fold it to my heart.

Decades pass – rummaging for something
I find a plastic bag – 'What's this?'
I open it – breathing stops
Daddy's bunnet, folded, waiting.

My eyes feast, my hand fears to touch,
Reverently I caress,
Hold it to my nose – no scent.
Long gone that perfume divine
I weep – the last touch of grief uncurls its fingers – lets go.

A tender smile of recognition,
His fragrance is in me now.
My inheritance – the biggest heart that ever beat
Pulses through my being.

I'm 64 now –
Even the briefest thought of his bunnet
Moves my soul, stirs my heart,
Melts me away
In a lifetime of love.

The Scotland I Support

Thomas Clark

It was back in the days when Scotland still used to qualify for the World Cup; not just for any World Cup but for all of them, always, and – as far as we knew – forever. A childhood of perennials, the eighties, when the monarch was always the queen, the prime minister always a woman, and the first round always the end of the line for Scotland.

Italia '90 was no different. In high hopes they went and in high dudgeon returned, the whole tournament spent teeter-tottering on the verge of extinction, like a clown on a high-wire. When finally they fell, it was as if the entire nation had had their hearts broken one too many times. Posters were binned, sticker albums abandoned, and the charity shops stuffed with replica shirts. The globalisation of the beautiful game was about to begin – Sky was happening, money was happening, and adherence to the creed of the merely local hero was a thing too parochial to be contemplated. Names started appearing on the back of shirts, shirts on the back of sponsors; and in playgrounds everywhere, our mad, one-upping race to spiritual and financial annihilation had begun.

It started when a boy in the year below showed up one day in a curious concoction of red, white and blue. Fascinated, we turned him around, passing him from hand to hand as he proudly boasted that his gran had got him it from Florida. It was the home shirt of the US national team, whose matches we'd never seen and players we'd never heard of. And it was sensational.

Week by week, the new and garish colours continued

to sprout up at our random kickabouts. The standard blues and greens thinned out and were replaced by dizzying arrays of neons, reds and purple hues. Japan, Jamaica, Fram Reykjavik of Iceland, the more obscure the shirt, the better – so long as they were up to date. Lad once showed up at a game with a Soviet Union strip on, a straight ten out of ten in anybody's book, except that the USSR had dissolved two years previously. He was sent home in disgrace, proper sine died. It was weeks before he had the nerve to show his face again, floating nervously above the collar of a Tunisia top – which, it was cruelly rumoured, was fake.

But shirts cost money, more money than most of us ever had. My mother, an absolute saint, had the native Scot's abhorrence of needless expense, and could not for the life of her see any reason to pay thirty quid for a football shirt when Oxfam had them for two pounds fifty. And so, whenever she spotted a shirt in a charity shop, she would snap it up for me immediately, without discrimination – and, it was always too small, and, it was always Scotland. Within a year of the World Cup I had enough shirts to put together a Scotland team of my own. They wouldn't have been much cop as set-pieces – my biggest shirt was a medium boys – but with me up front I reckon they'd have done alright. We'd have beaten Costa Rica, at least.

But nothing could have been so passé in those days as the age-old shirt of the country you were born in. Football seasons pass straight into history as soon as they are over, and their shirts with them, suddenly cringe-worthy and irrelevant. As for the idea of supporting your local or even national team, that was dead as soon as they started showing Italian football on Channel 4 on Sundays. To wear a two-year-old Scotland shirt was so counterculture that a cooler kid than I might even have set a trend. But I, alas, was not that kid, and was treated

15

instead with a mixture of scorn and pity – not because I was poor (we all were), but because I didn't seem to understand what was important in life, and what was important in life was a Fiorentina away shirt with the tags still on. It all reached a critical mass one day when a grasping hand at a free-kick tore my Scotland shirt from collar to hip. When I showed up the next day in an identical one, it slowly dawned on my peers that not only did I have the most ancient football shirt that any of them had ever seen, but I also seemed to have it in unlimited supply. A few friends gave up on me that day. There's some folks that, if they don't know, you can't tell 'em.

I still have those old shirts now, folded in the bottom of my bedroom cupboard, and would wear them again, if ever I recaptured the frame of a small, or even medium boy. It's not the only thing about being young I would like to have back again. They were austere times, just like ours, and the monarch was still a woman; but I never thought there'd be a 12-year-old boy in Scotland who wasn't born last time we played at a World Cup. I mean, I thought *I'd* have played at the World Cup by now. But I haven't, and neither have any of the other five million of us, not for a long time. Those shirts really are history now, history of a different kind, a social history, of a past when for three weeks each summer we all threw our lot in together and got in behind the idea of *us*. If there were to be winners, we would *all* be winners, and if (more likely) there were to be losers, well, that'd be us, too. No man left behind. No victory another man's defeat.

It was the World Cup in 1990, and Scotland had qualified. It's a long time ago now, but I still have the shirt. Because that's the Scotland I'm supporting. That's the Scotland I still hope will win.

16

Still Your Treasure...

Hannah Lavery

Still your treasure...

I keep it under my nighties. Folded like a secret under my big night shirts with the grinning cats. I keep it there to refer to, to remind myself, for when I think you look past me like a piece of the furniture, for when I look past myself.

For we rush by each other these days. We have dishes to be done, uniform to be found, children to placate. We swerve around each other as we tend to the endless chores. We speak to each other in half sentences. Our conversations have the substance of post-it notes and our kisses often miss the lips and land on already turning cheeks. Our 'I love you's are followed with 'will you?' and 'have you?' and we love in planned little chunks of time marked up on the calendar with the dentist appointments and parents evenings, but every night as I reach past my one sexy négligée for my big baggy nighties, I see it there, folded neat and if I have time I let the memory of it reach its way up to me.

The Clash were not of my time. I liked 'London Calling' but to be honest it was the T-shirt that I wanted. I can't remember where I had got it but it was that summer. Tight-fitting with a scooped neck, I wore it with jeans, in fact I wore it with everything. I remember if I bent low I would have your attention. It was the summer of late nights, of stolen looks. I wore other things but when we tell our story: the story we tell to new people we meet. The story we tell each other on anniversaries over dinner. You always mention how you remember me then, as that girl in The Clash T-shirt.

And now, I am three babies ruined and I buy things

that cover and drape. I hide myself in regret and promise myself new regimes, and when I feel bad and tell you I feel ugly or old, you say, that to you, I will always be that girl in The Clash T-shirt. And each night as I heave my now bigger and lumpier body into bed I take that image of my folded T-shirt with me too, and I fold that girl I was, into my sheets, tucking her up close.

Last year, when we had that huge row I had taken the T-shirt and thrown it away in one of those charity bags that come so often through the door. I dumped the bag on the kerb and stormed off down the road. Two hours later, I returned panicked and seeing the bag gone I was beside myself. You quickly took my hand and showed me the T-shirt returned to its place. You had shown me then a file marked *my life* on your computer. In it, a hundred photos; me holding our first wee boy hours after giving birth, in my wedding dress, on that holiday, my head peeping out of our first tent, covered in paint outside the door of this house, pregnant in a summer dress, that pint of Guinness you had with your brother in Barcelona, first days at school, Christmas mornings and of course, me, young, in love with you, in that Clash T-shirt, 'beautiful', you say. I look at you worried that I have grown into a disappointment and you, in your quiet voice, say 'beautiful, all of you, always'.

I do not have stacks of love letters, our romance has always existed in sideways glances, long walks home and in sitting too close as we listened to the gang around us. Our romance was in you taking too long to say anything and it was in me lingering too long as I bent down low to kiss you on your cheek and our romance now, is in the still, in the way you still see me, with those familiar eyes twinkling, in the way you still want me, as you did, although I lie by you in my big

18

baggy night shirt. Curled up close, with my sleepy head on your chest; curled up close, giggling with you and loving you like I did, when I leaned in, wrapped up like a present for you, beautiful, in my Clash T-shirt.

My T-shirt which lies like faded letters wrapped in a bow, like pressed flowers kept safe in scented paper, like photographs and trinkets in boxes. My T-shirt, neatly folded and safe in its place is our wee reminder, our treasure, our love graffiti, our names forever entwined.

Treasure on my Back

David McVey

The rucksack is an unsung masterpiece of design.
Everything you need, you carry on your back, while the
rucksack pulls your shoulders back and improves your
posture. Yet, for some reason, travellers have shifted en
masse to those vast, unstable, plastic suitcases on wheels
that crack the ankles of bystanders and are too broad to
run along train aisles or fit properly into luggage
compartments.

It's 1983 and I'm heading to Blair Atholl for some
hillwalking. Just as I'm leaving the house, my already
tatty rucksack literally falls from its frame, the stitching
rotted through. It's only six years old; mention of its
now-vanished make, Cobmaster, will provoke a
mirthless laugh from many veteran outdoor enthusiasts.

I quickly repack all my stuff into a couple of
supermarket plastic bags and hurtle off for the bus to
Glasgow. Once in town I make for Black's in St Vincent
Street (a long-gone branch) and quickly choose a new
rucksack; a Berghaus Delta 45, in thick, green
waterproof fabric with a sturdy internal frame and a
(then) revolutionary hip-belt with a quick-release buckle,
that enables you to spread the load from your shoulders
when required. It costs £41.95, a colossal amount in
1983, but I don't want to be left short by any other
Cobmaster-type rubbish. On the front step of Black's,
I haul the rucksack out of its billowing plastic bag and
hurl my gear into it. Then it's off to Queen Street
Station with minutes to spare.

Thirty years on I still have the same rucksack and it's
still in regular use. I couldn't begin to count the number
of trips to the wilds on which it's accompanied me

(overnight stays, day trips, longer expeditions in the hills) or, indeed, the number of high summits it's been to in Scotland, the Lakes, Yorkshire and Wales in all seasons. The rucksack has also accompanied me on holidays throughout the UK and to Austria and Switzerland and Belgium. Not only that, but my wife used it for a trip to Canada in the 1990s involving a wilderness canoe journey with a group of youngsters. A friend, then a student, borrowed it for her inter-railing trip around Europe about 1989, and in the late 1990s another friend took it to Tanzania so that youngsters on a youth camp there could use it when bivouacking. My rucksack is better travelled than I am.

It's still in great condition but the 45-litre capacity has been a bit constraining at times and at one point I actually splashed out on a larger replacement. However, the new sack on the block deteriorated quickly and I returned to the original and best and concentrated on travelling light.

Not long ago I had my first ever problem with it; one half of the buckle on the hip belt became detached and got lost. The hip belt was now unusable. The rucksack had been manufactured by Berghaus in their factory just over the border in Sunderland. The company still exists (unlike Cobmaster), even if they no longer manufacture in the UK, and so I emailed their customer service department explaining the hip-belt situation.

I was astonished to receive, through the post, entirely free of charge, a brand new buckle compatible with the hip belt. A quick, inexpensive repair job by a local outdoor shop and the rucksack really was as good as new. And with frightening speed I filled it with kit and set off for the Lakes for a sun-splashed February week on the Fells.

We get annoyed, rightly, when things don't last or work as they're supposed to, but perhaps we should show a similar intensity of positive reaction when things go right, and keep on going right, like my faithful rucksack has done for 30 years. Now, I know that a rucksack isn't something you can become emotionally attached to, nor is it something you'd display on a mantelpiece or in one of those glass-fronted cabinets for nick-nacks that our grandparents loved (not that it would fit in either case). But it's been with me on some of my most memorable experiences over three decades and I've also been able to lend it to others to enable them to get into remarkable places and have their own adventures. When it does all this without ever failing or breaking or letting me down, except in one minor, easily-remedied detail, then it becomes not just a valued possession, a treasure, but a silent sharer of dreams and passions.

I won't try again to replace my Berghaus Delta 45. I don't need to. In any case, it's become irreplaceable.

How Time Flies

Kay Ritchie

another infestation
tucks into a fine feast of fragrant fabrics
what a lick-lipping spread we've laid out on your bed –

seven decades of overcoats
cashmere pashminas and
a satin film-star pyjama suit

the search is on for tell-tale eggs

down seams
under arms
inside collars

this black felt hat emerged
ruched with a bow and
bunched French butterfly lace
(silk stockings stuffed inside)

perfect
as that day of you in crushed raspberry
with black velvet collar and
three-inch high suede courts

suddenly memories like tiny silver wings let loose
the Baptist church
the best-maid Elsie
John West's salmon sandwiches spread thing from
one saved-up ration book tin and
a Craig's bakery cake that lacked fruit
its icing sugar – hard cardboard

there should be four more black hats
worn on the sombre occasions which had still to come
all now gone to feed the moths but

this one will survive as we toss
in generous amounts of cedar and lavender
it will be treasured
forever

The Pyjama Genie

Carolyn Roberts

My pyjamas are white, patterned with blue and yellow teddy bears. They are saggy, and they smell funny.

The smell is not surprising: they are over 14 years old. Plus, when I was a student and did not possess a washing machine, I'd regularly start laundering them in the bath, get bored and leave them sitting in water for a week.

I last wore them around 1998, but I can't throw them away. They are the last thing that my mum gave me before she died.

Obviously, she didn't plan it that way. It wasn't like there was an emotional deathbed scene during which she ceremoniously presented me with a set of teddy bear jammies. She happened to give them to me, and then she happened to get ill. Life is like that, sometimes.

Mum gave me many other things, none of which I have kept. There was the silver ring that I wore every day for years. The ill-advised sparkly purple dress that I eventually decided not to wear for my 21st birthday party (I wore a silver, sequined, even-less-well-advised one instead). The books she bought me for my university course in Scottish Literature. Every term, I'd send Mum the reading list and she'd post each book to me one at a time, always reading them herself first. Each book would be accompanied by a letter in her quirky, sardonic style, telling me what she thought of the book and imparting domestic news about the cat, my dad and the new dishwasher.

Where are all those things? Why didn't I treasure them? Why didn't I take each mundane trinket she gave me and wrap it carefully in tissue paper, storing it away against the unimaginable day that she would no longer be there? Because it was unimaginable, that's why. If I thought about it at all, I assumed that day would come in a distant future in which Mum was very, very old and I was completely equipped to handle her death.

It turns out the future comes sooner than you expect it. She wasn't old and I wasn't equipped. I wasn't equipped at all. You could, of course, argue that the physical items Mum gave me are meaningless. The real gifts she gave me are innate. Mum is in every gesture I make and every word I write. She gave me:

- her habit of rolling her eyes at unreasonable people
- her inability to stop shouting at politicians on the television
- her love of words, books and language
- her tendency to put on a TV newsreader voice when answering the phone
- her chronic short-sightedness

I can remember my mum simply by looking in the mirror, but that's not enough. I want stuff. I want things I can hold in my hand and be comforted by.

It is odd, this business of remembering people by things. We look at a vase on the mantelpiece and think of Great Aunty Audrey. The item becomes the repository of their being. It is the bottle we rub to make their genie come out. But why? After all, we don't forget people just because we've nothing that they owned. If you want the whole world to remember you, then yes, you probably need to leave behind a monument, an invention or a building with your name on it. But if all you're after is for your own children to remember you, then bequeathing objects to them shouldn't matter.

I am filled with memories of my mum. Some are painful, some make me laugh, some leave me puzzled.

I wouldn't forget any of them if I lost those fousty old pyjamas, so why do I value them so highly? Why do we cling on to these pointless old relics?

I think it's because they make us feel joined to our loved one again. Looking at something upon which the person we've lost has also gazed unites us, in a funny way. It's a way of sharing space with people once we can never again share time with them.

Mum's death brought about many 'firsts'. My first day back at work after the funeral. The first time I read a book and couldn't discuss it with her. The first Christmas, when Dad and I tried hard but could find little to celebrate. In the 14 years since she died there have been so many 'first times' that almost nothing about me is the same as when Mum died.

There are hardly any items in my home that would be familiar to her. She never met my partner and she wouldn't know my daughter. The truth is, that scares me. The ridiculous, embarrassing truth is, I still don't believe Mum is not coming back. And I am frightened she might not recognise me if she did.

And that's why I keep the pyjamas. So that there is something one tiny, ludicrous object — that Mum would find familiar. If I met her again, I could offer her the sour, fading cloth and say 'Mum, look, it's me'.

Tools

Winnie's Tea Caddy

Denise Mina

My treasure is my tea caddy.

It is an old Co-op biscuit tin in grey metal with blue and yellow decorations painted on it. It's much faded, much battered, with a good-fitting lid to keep the tea bags fresh. The paint has worn off around the handle where fingers have pinched once, twice, ten times a day for 40 or 50 years, pulling the lid off, taking out a tea bag, fitting it back on. That wear and tear has eroded the paint. It has exposed a silver base coat underneath and finally the base grey metal the tin is made from.

On the bottom, in industrial type, it says:

UNITED CO-OPERATIVE BAKING SOCIETY LTD
Glasgow Clydebank Belfast

The tin came from my gran, Winnie's house, after she died. It was faded and worth nothing and no one else wanted it.

Winnie and I never liked each other. She was not an especially warm woman, but even allowing for that, we never liked each other. My earliest memories of her involve us being left alone in a kitchen and tacitly agreeing to pretend the other wasn't there.

She was capable of warmth: she adored my big sister. When we were very small and sleeping at her house, she would get into the double bed we were sleeping in with a tray of Rose's lime-marmaladed toast and a wet flannel. She always sat close to my sister and I was miles out on the edge of the bed, watching them eat and giggle and wipe the sticky jam from their hands.

I could lie and say the space between us was a source

of sadness to me, or her, or both of us, but the truth is always better: that is how it was and we weren't much bothered. In big, big families there is always a sub for any position. Really, I had my Auntie Betty for granny-warmth and constancy.

But Winnie and I spent a lot of time together. Wherever we went in the world she would come and stay for months at a time. I can't remember a conversation with her that wasn't about finishing my dinner or her telling me about 'ladies'. They didn't have a lot of scope for movement, ladies. Poor things.

A lady, said Winnie, doesn't rub her mouth with her napkin, a lady *dabs* her mouth at the corners. There were a hundred lady dos and don'ts in my childhood and Winnie always put on a strange, strangled sort of voice as she imparted them. Don't sniff. Don't look in the mirror. Don't bend down in the street to look at chewing gum patterns on a hot pavement. Don't shout at dogs. Don't eat Nutella with a spoon. Basically, whatever I was doing at any given moment was what ladies don't do. Poor ladies.

Ours wasn't an actively hostile relationship. It wasn't spiteful and she was certainly never mean to me. I think I was a bit mean to her. I got a witch puppet when I was five and called it Winnie. I rolled my eyes when she told me about these ladies. I dodged her. I didn't visit when she was dying.

Winnie had mental health issues, spent a bit of time in a psychiatric hospital, was on mysterious medicine that made her slur in the evenings. She always seemed a bit fragile but she was proud, too.

When she was a young lady Winnie wore fox fur stoles. She teased her hair into a bouffant as high as a stove pipe hat and trained as a French polisher. It was highly skilled, a seven-year apprenticeship. She had to

31

give up work as soon as she got married. Ladies didn't work. She left her home in Bressie Road, Barlanark to travel the world, Paris, San Francisco, visiting relatives, maybe giving them advice about being a lady.

Winnie and I didn't like each other. That's how it was and there was nothing we could do about it.

But we both liked this United Co-operative Baking Society tin. Both of us used this tin every day. Once, twice, ten times a day, Winnie and I heard the inverted kiss of a vacuum lid come off –pwuff. Once, twice, ten times a day, we felt the warmth of a nice wee cup of tea in our hands.

And possibly a biscuit.

Ma Coal Fire

Liz Niven

Efter A'd been askt tae write aboot a traisure, A wis gazin intae ma coal fire in a dwam and wunnerin whit is an important thing tae me. An A thocht tae masel, It's this. Ma traisure is ma coal fire. Nae wunner it's cried black gowd. Precious jist the same.

Whit amazes me is the wey, wi ma coal fire, every sense is active. Thir's the soond o crackle and hiss, the feelin o warmth oan yer skin, the reek o smoke rich an pungent, sometimes even the taste o it oan yer mooth. An the sicht o yella an reid an blue flames is mesmeric, hypnotic an a fine focus when ye're dreamin yer ain thochts oan a caul winter day or nicht.

Thir's nacthin like ma coal fire livin awa in ma hoose. Especially fir a writer, or oniebodie that enjoys a wee bit o solitary time. Ma coal fir is like a pet in ma hoose. Ye're no on yer ain, thir's somethin needin attendin tae noo an then. It doesnae demand a lot o attention but ye need tae feed it or it'll no keep gaun. An sae it's lik a companion. A kinna quiet wan.

It's wan o the maist primitive, primeval things, fire. An coal has taen millions o years tae be made. Sometimes it seems ridiculous that, efter aw the years in the makin, A jist burn it aw awa. Kinna scary it cannae be replaced verra easily. Maks it aw the mair precious an aw. Aye, A love ma coal fire.

Like watter, it's a life-giver and life-taker. It maks its ain decisions. Gans its ain wey. It has a fascination unique tae itsel.

In ilka hoose A've lived in, A made sure A had a coal fire. Even wan hoose A flitted tae that didnae hiv wan, the wumman had boardit it up, A brung in the man fae

33

the local fireplace shop and he said, 'Nae problem, missus, A can pit the fire back in'. The only problem was, there wis nae chimney. A fire wi'oot a lum. A happent tae hiv wan, (as ye dae...) a lovely auld clay yella wan, brung fae the hoose A'd jist flitted fae. It had been an auld Victorian school hoose and this auld lum had been on an oothoose. It got shoogly an dangerous an A had tae bring it doon. It made a brilliant gairden feature an A plantit flooers in it.

So, A had the coal shop mannie pit this lum on the roof, open up the fireplace and it wis aw workin great. Then wan summer, somebody says tae me, 'Whit's that stickin oot o yer chimney?' A dashed oot tae look an a muckle sunflooer wis growin oot o it. It must've still had some seeds fae the days it wis in the gairden. It wis like a wee bondin fae wan hoose tae the ither, wan fire tae anither. Coal sometimes seems lik a livin thing.

A wis daein a scuil projeck recentlie in a pairt o Scotlan that was ex-minin. The lan wis bein 'regeneratit'. The weans wir studyin the life o coal miners and they had a box o artefacks fae the museum. Wan wee boy came up tae me wi something tichtlie grasped in his haun. 'Look whit A've got', he said proodlie. 'Wid ye like a bit tae keep?' An in his wee haun he had a lump o coal. He'd fun it in his gairden and seen it as a gey special thing. A traisure. A thanked him kindly, taen it carefully lik it wis a precious stone an didnae liek tae tell him A had a coal bunker wi a few hunner wecht o these at hame.

Wance A lived in a cauld auld school house in the Highlands. Nae central heatin, east coast winds whuppin throu the doors an windaes. The coal fire wis a God. Ye worshipped it. An ye didnae let it go oot at any time. Even ower nicht we fun a wey o fillin plastic milk cartons an tin cans wi dross (wee tottie pieces o coal sma as peas) an bankin the fire up. In the morning, a reid sky shinin ower the Machar Mhor an a wee wean greetin fir it's breakfast, ye'd gie the fire a dunt wi the lang steel poker an it wid leap intae bricht warm flames. So wid yer hairt. So tae speak.

Fire an lums is attractive tae birds an aw. A mind wance the smoke wis reekin oot intae the livin room an it wis jackdaws nestin oan wire mesh stopping the smoke fae gettin up an oot. An the mesh had been pit there tae stop them comin doon the lum, sae they jist parked thirselves oan tap o the mesh. *Cannae shift us that easily,* they must've thocht.

Sometimes, ma haun reaches oot tae the coal scuttle tae pit mair coal on the fire, nae gloves. A like the feel o the dustiness an grit unner ma palm. An if fir a minute, A don't like the durt, A mind on the miners deep unner grun, black dark aw day, sookin in danger aw day or even mind the mannie deliverin ma coal who shunts this muckle bag oan his back, an gie a minute's thocht tae whit they risk jist tae gie me ma heat an comfort. A weird contrast the cauld coal pit tae ma room bricht an flickerin wi warmth.

A suppose even in folk lore and in idioms and metaphors (metafires ...!) fire is a sign of somethin. Bad or guid. 'Nae reek in the laverock's hoose' – bad or 'lang ma yer lum reek' – guid.

Sae it's mibbe an odd traisure, bit traisure's sic a personal thing, is it no? The philosopher Kahlil Gibran said, 'Perhaps time's definition of coal is the diamond'. A like that. A think oan that when A'm starin intae ma fire.

If ye fling away the 'h' in hearth ye get 'heart'. An tae me ma coal fire's like a pulsin hairt, livin an breathin an warm. Life-gien. Black gowd.

Dad's Bargain

Linda Brown

Mum was revamping her bedroom. A complete wall to wall make-over – out with the 1950s, heavy, brown furniture and in with sleek, modern rosewood units.

Her double wardrobe, a wedding gift from her grandparents, stuffed to bursting with clothes, shoes, accessories and mementos accumulated and salted away over decades took us hours to empty and declutter. And it was in that old wardrobe, tucked away in a dark corner of the top shelf behind Mum's emergency stock of embroidered pillowcases and tablecloths that I rediscovered my late father's pride and joy. His treasure.

At first glance it was nothing special, just a plain chestnut brown case holding an old fashioned and outmoded camera. But at over 50 years old the case was in remarkably good condition (just slightly scuffed) and still held the faint scent of fresh leather, whilst the camera inside, a German-made Agfa Isolette, appeared clean and well cared for. So precious was this object to my dad that as a child I was never allowed to touch it let alone use it. Now my finger itched to press the little silver button which would reveal its lens. Dare I…? The bellows sprang out like a jack-in-the-box liberated after years of incarceration and the lens mechanism snapped securely into place. Pressing my eye to the viewfinder I framed my mother.

'We can't throw that out.' Her voice quavered.

Dad acquired his treasure second-hand in Iraq. He was stationed there at RAF Habbaniya during 1957 while completing his National Service. A fellow aircraft fitter, a young Englishman and the Isolette's original owner, short of cash and desperate for beer money for his weekend leave had been trying to flog his camera around the billet. No one but Dad had shown any interest in buying what at that time was considered an expensive, luxury item. An item he'd previously admired with envy. So a price was negotiated – 'a bargain' Dad always maintained – hands were shaken and Dad took possession of his first camera and, as the complete dearth of photographs from his childhood attests, probably the first camera in his family. His next leave was spent familiarising himself with the workings of the Isolette and photographing scenes around the base. Mum still cherishes a leather-bound album filled with the small black and white images taken in Iraq and from his subsequent postings in Cyprus and Libya.

For almost thirty years this camera recorded my family's lives. From his courtship of my mother, their February honeymoon in a freezing Edinburgh, their first summer holiday together on the Isle of Man to my arrival the following year; wherever he went, whatever family event we attended, Dad took his camera. An image of him with its case slung casually over his shoulder is imprinted on my memory clearer than any enhanced photograph. Our albums bulge with prints of me on my birthday, Mum wearing her 'lamp shade' hat at a wedding, his first car – an old Morris Minor, countryside picnics, seaside paddles and trips to the zoo. Towards the end of the sixties and just in time for the birth of my sister, he upgraded to colour film which had formerly been outwith his budget. And the photos continued to roll out – my sister and I at Southport – Mum and I giggling on the 'Cups and Saucers' ride at the Pleasure Beach – me, a surly teenager scowling next to Mons Meg at Edinburgh Castle and my sister, ever the tomboy, saluting on the ramparts. He captured us on the beach at Barassie, Blackpool then Benidorm.

Dad used the Isolette right up to the mid 1980s

when he succumbed to temptation and replaced it with a Canon Sure Shot. That camera and its successors have long since been consigned to the dustbin or charity shop, but Dad could never bear to part with his Isolette. It meant too much to him.

So, of course, Mum and I didn't throw the camera out that day. How could we? Although it holds no great monetary value, to us it is priceless. And now Dad's treasure is my treasure. The camera resides with me, nestling on the top shelf of my wardrobe surrounded by the clothes I always mean to slim into.

Today's rapidly changing digital technology – Smartphones, iPhones, iPads, Androids – has rendered Dad's camera and others like it obsolete. Glossy photographs are no longer arranged then fixed and neatly captioned in albums. Now images are stored on computer memories, discs or flashdrives. The patience and skill required to fit a roll of film, snap 24 exposures without the ability to delete, then rewind and carefully remove the film out of direct light are qualities heading for extinction. As for waiting for days before collecting prints and negatives from the developers... well, who wants to do that when you can view your pictures with the click of a mouse?

The Isolette will soon be a museum piece, a snapshot from the past.

But this summer I've bought a spool of black and white film. My treasure is coming out of retirement and I can't wait to see the results.

Spot On

Finola Scott

When I touched it
base metal
deep in the drawer.
I knew it – Dad's plumb-line,
a tool that built brochs and battlements

In the string's strands I smelt
Dad's sweet sweat
stood beside him again
as wallpaper and brick were ruled
with ease and ancient science.

He'd unravel the tawny twine
from the dull weight
that held the cord sure
then
drop.

It swung out
Tic
Toc
Tic
down
to a calm
stop.

He smiled and explained gravity.
I listened and nibbled Newton's apple.
Our home safe in his hands
his judgement always true.

My Grandfather's Pocket Knife

Nacho Vinuela

My granddad never went anywhere without his pocket knife. It was always in his pocket and it came in handy whenever he had to cut a piece of string or loosen a screw; the point of the blade got bent, because you're not really meant to use it as a screwdriver. He used it to trim the wicker when he was weaving baskets or to peel apples in the family orchard when they were ripe. He would offer me a juicy slice on the blade of his pocket knife and waited patiently until I swallowed before he carved another one with a raspy sound. The apples never tasted better than when eaten like that and I would stubbornly ignore them once they were piled up in the fruit bowl. More likely than not, my granddad would be telling a story while he was slicing the fruit. Granddad had a way with words. His stories were as tasty as his apples.

He often told us the story of how, in the dark times after the Spanish Civil War, he got into trouble because of his pocket knife. He was cycling in the dark, on his way to a party in a nearby village. He had his bike's light off in order to escape attention because you were not allowed to travel at night without a safe-conduct. There weren't many opportunities to have a good time back then, and he really wanted to go to this party. He was 16 when the war ended. I had never been to parties like those, he said. So there he was, cycling with his best clothes on, when the Guardia Civil stepped onto the road in front of him. He dismounted. Fearing a body search, he tried to hide his pocket knife under the seat of his bike, but it fell off. One of the officers stooped, picked it up, and without a word slapped my granddad twice across the face. At this point in the story he always laughed, although his eyes narrowed in a wince as if he could still feel the pain and the humiliation of the blows.

'It didn't put me off from going to parties, though,' he would say, amused, 'and thank God for that, as I met your granny at one. She shone like an angel despite those horrible mourning clothes they made her wear. How we danced!'

No matter how sad his stories were there was always a touch of humour, a sense of wonder, an opening for hope. It was through my granddad's storytelling that I came to appreciate the conjuring power of words, both the ability to bring something to mind and to perform magic.

As I write down his words I can hear the husky and warm sound of his voice. Writing about him, I bring him back from death.

I travelled to Spain when my granddad had by-pass surgery. He was unconscious when I went into the ICU. His chest rose abruptly every time the artificial ventilator inflated his lungs. The skin of his face looked waxy and his eyes were closed and sunken. His big, knobbly hands looked desolately idle on the bed sheet. They looked like they'd rather be doing something. I held one of them in mine for a few moments. I would have liked to have said something but I felt intimidated by the hiss of the ventilator and the beeping of the monitors.

My granddad survived the surgery and a few days later he was making us all laugh with his stories. My granny smuggled an apple into his room and he lamented not having his pocket knife at hand.

I returned to Scotland with the resolution of visiting him more often and writing down his stories so they would never be lost.

He died a week later of a lung infection. It did not make sense. That wasn't the way the tale should have gone. It was crap storytelling. I didn't go to his funeral. My family told me there was no point. I was lucky to have seen him happy and full of hope, they said. Lucky to have such a good last memory of him. But because I didn't scatter his ashes into the sea, I couldn't really mourn him. My grief was a stone in my chest.

A few days later I received an envelope from my mother. Inside was my granddad's pocket knife. They had found it in the last pair of trousers he had worn. It was smaller than I remembered it. Seeing it folded in on itself, like a cat sleeping in his master's absence, I felt a stab of sadness. I placed it on the palm of my hand. The wooden handle felt warm and was shiny from use. I opened it and smelled the groove. It smelled like the inside of hazelnuts. The blade was scratched and its edge was so sharp it was nearly transparent (my granddad kept it sharp using a filing stone). The engraved name of the place where the pocket knife was made (the mythological-sounding 'Taramundi') was faded. I don't know for how long I was looking at it, turning it around this way and that, running the tip of my finger along its edge, trying to decipher its long history. I felt it was all there, every memory of my granddad was in it. I put it in my pocket and went for a walk to the beach. As I stood looking at the waves, I could hear my granddad's voice: 'You never know when it might come in handy. Let me tell you a story…'

Recreation

Treasured Ted

Mairi Hedderwick

The treasure was never a treasure in the beginning; it was just an old unloved teddy bear.

The bear was given to my mother for her new and only baby before I was born. Why did my mother have to tell me that? Who gave it to her? I think it came from relatives belonging to the wealthier side of the family. He had a barred nursery-window look to him. I don't think he was a Steiff bear but he was certainly stiff. Metal swivels attached tight straw-filled limbs to a solid straw-stuffed body. Not at all cuddly by today's foam-filled standards.

He was of his time. My mother when asked my age would say without fail that I was born in May '39 and war was declared in September. I grew up knowing it was all my fault.

Ted gave me no comfort. Vacant, amber glass eyes, a black stitched snout and a little peevish mouth gave him a quizzically sad expression. I meticulously cut off his fur one day, his skin exposed and goosebumped forever.

I have one vivid memory of caring for Ted when we were both about five years old. Friends were visiting with their son and daughter. We children were left to play in the sitting room. The boy proceeded to violently bounce Ted repeatedly along the back of the couch, laughing at me all the while, ignoring my weeping remonstrations. His sister egged him on.

War gave way to peace and bananas and Dinky Toys. Ted sat isolated on a shelf in my bedroom watching over the many years I collected the tiny farm machinery

44

and livestock. The hens were very dinky. The farmer with a smock was a bit strange. His sheepdogs and bucket-carrying wife were the dinkiest. The removable tractor driver – their son, of course – would sometimes be seated on a matchstick gate staring out over our landed estate.

The floral squared Axminster bedroom carpet totalled the hectares of my farm in winter but summer days in the garden were best. The crazy paving became in-by fields linked by weaving cement roads that edged the meadows of the sloping lawn; spent matchsticks and thread fencing further delineated areas for grass cutting and haymaking.

Next on the list of obsessions came tiny glass animals, a mantelpiece laden with them. They glistened like Ted's ever watchful eyes. Then it was postage stamps and walking the dog up on the Heather Hill for endless hours. And then it was time to grow up.

Strange to say when I left home Ted came with me and continued to watch from the sidelines, albeit from the back of a cupboard, the rites of passage of college, marriage and parenting.

By now all my ambitions were fulfilled even unto the cows, the sheep and driving the tractor. It was Ted's turn; his rehabilitation assured by the arrival of my children. They would love him as I never had.

They did not.

The traditional dump for our home on the south side of the island was a cleft in the north side cliffs. The sea slurped below but never could be seen. There the trailer tipped down accumulated unrecyclable junk. It was a family ritual that belonged to an era before council collections and, in my defence, before the plethora of plastic packaging.

The rebuilding of the old house was finished.
The children's rooms painted, curtained and carpeted.
New toys nestled in cupboards.

Ted sat on top of the dump-run junk. He got a great
cheer when he slid into the ravine.

Why was I party to this? Was I, like the little boy of
long ago, enjoying bullying Ted with cruel laughter and
in so doing ridding myself of a childhood trauma?

Six months later, walking along a beach near to the
dump, there was Ted washed up. Intact, save one eye,
his sodden being was joyously carried home and
ceremoniously perched above the stove to dry out.
The sea-soaked straw and fabric never lost their salty
dampness so he remained there *ad infinitum* and was
the toast of many a dinner party. His remaining benign
eye looked kindly on us all.

Ad infinitum is not always forever. In time a slow sadness
came over the house and the family within. A crazed
splinter was starting to shatter the dream. It was
decided that leaving the island would seal the cracks.

The house was sold. There were many runs to the
dump. No cheers when Ted, now disgustingly mouldy,
sat atop the last trailer load and fell into the sea. It was
my decision, the appropriate finale to all things childish.

Life on the mainland was healing but I would go
back to the island and privately mourn every summer.

And the second summer? Washed up on the high
winter tide line of a beach on the island's south coast lay
the remains of old Ted. His one-eyed head and one
solitary arm held together by a fankle of threads woven
around four rusty metal joints. He lay, tinder dry, in a
nest of dried marram grass.

How had he got there? By half circumnavigating the
island? And why washed up just below the house that
I stayed in for holidays?

Both of us are mainlanders now. The island that kept calling us back, on and off, for over 40 years – he in his shoebox tied with a blue silk ribbon and me with obsessional house moves – has finally let us go.

Ted is now a famous bear redeemed in the Katie Morag story *Katie Morag and the Tiresome Ted*. He is her treasure of treasures. It is the least I can do for him.

He still refuses to answer any of my questions, however.

Grafonola

Beatrice Colin

I inherited one of my most precious treasures, a
Columbia Grafonola, from the 1920s, from my Great
Aunt Nina. Although the box looks scruffy, like an old,
unloved suitcase, with a worn, leather carrying handle
and scuffed edges, inside, its chrome and blue velvet
turntable looks brand new. In a pocket are half a dozen
pristine 78s. As well as 'Night and Day' and 'There's an
Old Hotel', for some reason my aunt had the Peruvian
National Anthem.

Every time I give the crank a dozen turns, choose
some music and carefully place the needle on the record,
I'm amazed at the sound that comes out. The volume
(unadjustable) is a blast of pure, glorious joy. The music,
recorded live, has so much energy, so much zip, that you
want to get up and dance. It's like being transported
back to a brighter, simpler world.

My great aunt, however, did not have a simple life.
She was born in Russia and left during the revolution
aged about 19. After living in Berlin and working in the
film industry, she moved to Paris and worked for the
producer Alexander Korda. Her husband, Walter, was
also a film producer and in the late twenties and early
thirties, they lived a glamorous life of film premiers and
cocktail parties. Their flat was featured in Paris *Vogue*,
they drove a Citroen Convertible and spent the summer
in Nice wearing the latest fashion.

When the war broke out, however, their life changed.
Nina was Jewish and Walter was German. He joined the
Free French in Algeria and she was interned. Having a
German name saved her from gas chambers but not

from spending several years in a prison camp as an enemy alien. Finally she was released and spent the remainder of the war in Algeria.

Afterwards, the film industry changed. Many of their friends and colleagues had moved to America or perished. When neither she nor her husband could find work, Nina started a business making things for the home out of fabric. Her biggest commission was producing thousands of red roses made from handkerchiefs for Air France.

By the time I met her, Walter had been dead for years. She lived in a small flat in the 16th arrondissement in Paris in a flat that had seen better days, and survived on a diet of vegetable soup, chocolate and champagne. This suited her, as although she had taken a decade off her age when she had entered France in the 1920s, by our family's calculation, she lived to be 100.

In my 20s, I accompanied her on holiday several times to Cannes and Cabourg in Normandy. Afterwards she would demand regular updates on my then disastrous love life. Her solution was that I should probably wear more make-up.

When she died, my father, aunt and I went to Paris for her funeral. As she wasn't religious, we read out a passage by Chekov and placed a bunch of mimosa, her favourite flower, on her coffin.

Afterwards, we had a day to clear her flat. As was the custom in France, she had sold it to a couple 30 years earlier in exchange for an allowance for the rest of her life. She had lived so long, however, that the husband was already dead and his widow eager for access.

Nina, it seemed as we began to empty the contents of her drawers, kept everything. We filled bin bag after bin bag with old cheque receipts, some of which dated from the 1950s. There were also volumes of photographs, dozens of rolls of film, Venetian glass lamps, plus pictures, clothes and ornaments.

I wanted to take it all but since I was travelling home by train, I couldn't. I packed Walter's dinner suit and a few books of photographs. My aunt, who lives in Rome, arranged for a few of the more valuable pieces to be shipped. The rest would be sold or binned.

My eye had passed over the Grafonola several times. I thought it was a suitcase and dreaded finding more things to sort through and throw away. And then I opened it.

It wasn't easy to take the Grafonola home on the Eurostar. Although it is fairly small, it is really heavy. Each of the 78s, for example, weighs about a pound. And I had a dozen. By the time I had braved the London underground in the rush hour and walked half a mile from the bus stop to reach the flat I was living in, my shoulders ached and I had blisters on both hands. Of course, I never regretted it.

I love the Grafonola for two reasons. Most of the music I listen to involves a couple of clicks of a mouse or pressure on a button. The sound quality is excellent; the acoustics perfect. To play the Grafonola involves physical effort. You have to crank it up and if it runs out of power half way through a song, it will slow down and stop unless you wind it up again. I love placing the needle in a groove and don't care about the scratches and the hiss. It is music that sounds alive in a way that recorded music so often doesn't. It almost breathes.

I also love it because it captures a time in Nina's life when everything was going well. She was young, successful and judging by the photographs, happy. As a soundtrack to another life, the music is simply a celebration.

Colours of the Wind

Bethany Ruth Anderson

The wind wasn't painted many colours at the top of the coal bing. So far as I could see, everything was green or grey. Beneath my feet, broken slate shifted brown. With a hand over my eyes I could squint into the distance to seek ships sailing into harbour. Instead, my landscape was green field or grey schemes. But this was a perilous journey, tiptoed on the precipice of a great cliff. Eyes closed, I could inhale the scents of my dead ancestors through the breeze. Everything about being there was dangerous, because I might fall and the stones would rip my face off. Mum said she'd seen that before, in a hospital, a boy with half his face missing because he went where he was told not to go. Probably, that boy had gone away on his own. Probably, he hadn't gone with a Native American princess.

Pocahontas held onto my hand, keeping me safe. Her hands were much smaller than mine, with a perfect manicure. Her fingers were stuck together, but she still had a good grip. My eyes were small and blue, but hers were wide brown almonds, all the better to see the beautiful world she lived in. On her arm was a red tribal tattoo, and her legs were slender, with strong calves, and pointed toes, so that she could keep alert. Even her clothes were beautiful, and practical for swimming in lakes and jumping off cliffs. Best of all, the material was magical. If I held her tiny body in my hands and lifted her high above my head, then the sun would bring out small gold leaves on her dress. Pocahontas knew she was the most beautiful princess doll in my collection, but she didn't let on. She was the only doll not coupled

51

with a handsome prince. She was the only doll that didn't try to run away from her family. Mostly, she was the only one with guts enough to adventure far, far away with me.

Way up here, we could duet our way through her soundtrack without anyone complaining. We both knew all the words to all the other princesses' soundtracks too. The top of the bing was for singing the loudest. Up here, we could even choreograph the songs with tearaway glances and outstretched arms. When the dust moved beneath our feet, we knew it was time to stop the ballet lessons. Even if Pocahontas was here to protect me, we didn't want to be the 'boy with no face'. I imagined us tucked up in a hospital bed, her eyes scratched from her plastic face, my cheek completely pulled away. We would cry together and sing about how sorry we were, we both just wanted to be free. Why was the fighting happening? They just didn't understand us as a people. The bing was where we belonged, that was all.

But we could tiptoe our way down from the bing, though it did sometimes involve me shuffling on my bum, getting my leggings dirty with tell-tale signs of red ash. Pocahontas would sit on my lap, warning me to be careful of the big swirling pit where the boys sometimes took their dirt bikes. The walk home went round the back of the primary school, past the park where the paedophile went who would later turn out just to be a rumour so a group of kids could get the park to themselves, along the road past a house where a man lived who would later kill himself in prison, past where the Bogey Boy used to live who would sneeze gelatinous green across my desk at school, down the scheme past the house where the mad lady lived and her gypsy husband who used to bleed on her doorstep, and across the road at the house where a prostitute did business while her child slept in the next room, and through the gate to my house. My house, where I lived with Pocahontas, a younger brother, and a baby sister who came from my step-dad, who had married my mum.

On the top bunk in my bedroom, Pocahontas and I swung our legs over the wooden edge, paddling our feet in the cool, steady river. We spoke in conspiratorial whispers, about whether the mad lady would actually kill her gypsy husband like she said, about what flavour of yoghurt to have after dinner, about how late my father would be when he picked me up on Saturday. Pocahontas had said herself that inanimate objects had life and spirits, and likely she knew that she was no exception. This meant that we could be friends, and that she could be inseparable with me. Friends that we were, she would eat dinner with me, watch herself and the other princesses on television with me, splash in the bath with me (though she never liked getting her hair wet) and she would even come to the cinema with me, sneaking in without a ticket.

When my new dad sang, 'Skinny malinky long legs big banana feet, went to the pictures and fell through the seat' and everybody laughed, perhaps he didn't think about how Pocahontas was skinnier and malinkier than me. I imagined her sitting at the bottom of someone's seat at the ABC, stuck in darkness forever, never able to see the gold leaves appearing on her dress, forced to watch films that she didn't even like. But even worse was the idea that another little boy or girl might have taken her home to play with. Eight years old, and I had to learn to let go of dark straw hair, a perfectly symmetrical face, rubbery legs, and tiny plastic fingers and toes. Big girls didn't need dolls, and I could grow up without her.

Still, whatever little girl had her now, they wouldn't know that what made Pocahontas happier than anything in all the world was to stand at the top of the coal bing and sing.

My Finding Treasure

Nicole Brandon

My treasure isn't what you find in the sunken pirate
ship, it's what you need to find the sunken pirate ship.
You don't need a map, or a boat, or a metal detector, or
a tantalising fragment of some unclaimed golden hoard.
Those things are great but what you need to find
anything down there is a way of seeing underwater.

When I was seven we paid a family fortune for my
second diving mask. Twenty-five dollars (plus six per
cent Florida sales tax) from the dive shop on the corner
of Forest Hill and Congress, which would've been my
favourite store if I'd ever thought of it as a store. It was a
neon-lit cave on stilts, full of snorkel, tank and
freediving gear and the air inside was warm and heavy,
mottled with breathing mixture seeping from re-filled
SCUBA tanks. It was the same place my first mask came
from, which made the shopping trip feel like going back
to the Techno Pro Sub Aqua family homestead and
telling them their eldest son had been lost at sea, could I
take the next in line, please?

Of course, that's exactly what I did: cheerily picked
the first one right off the hook, the blue one. My little
brother snagged the one next to it, a red one.

We were replacing gear lost in a capsize that nearly
lost us, too. I suppose we could have gotten therapy, or
a month's worth of steak dinners, but instead we were
at the dive shop trying on replacement fins, snorkels and
masks – the most expensive stuff we could afford.
Because, without fail, when it comes to diving gear you
get what you pay for. You can't say that for everything.

Twenty-five dollars and tax, then. My second mask

was bought adult sized at the adult price because I had an adult head, and I've had this mask all my adult life. It's got a tempered glass faceplate, a lifetime guarantee vinyl skirt seal, a blue hard plastic frame and a neon neoprene strap designed not to snag in long wet hair.

Neither the strap nor the frame have faded in 20 years of ocean-going with me, and I don't expect they ever will. My mask does have some wear and tear (mostly damage it took protecting my too-curious face) and, inexplicably, there's sand wedged inside around the edge of the faceplate, pressed under glass like a museum exhibit. The mask weighs enough to hurt if you swing it at someone on purpose, and it smells like the salt of every single dive it's seen with me.

Which is probably why I can put it on, think for a moment, and remember all the things I've ever seen through it without trying. Not just that, but I can remember what it felt like to see them, clear and perfect on the other side of the glass.

On a dive, my mask was an aquarium with just my eyes inside. Looking out under the sea from behind glass, and being looked at by everything at home in a place I couldn't otherwise be. My mask was the means of my incredible explorations, and all it did was contain a pocket of air over my eyes and nostrils. That was its job, and it did it well – excepting the times we didn't get along.

Second time out I sneezed in it, and glued my left eyelid shut with snot while I was freediving 20 feet under the surface. (Not fun, but everybody laughed.) Another time, I didn't spit-rinse it right, and it fogged up completely as me and my best friend tag-teamed a lobster we were hell-bent on eating. (It's just getting fatter out there, we'll catch it one day.)

One time, I smiled so wide my dimples broke the

mask's seal with my face and it flooded. I was watching a bright yellow sea slug dancing itself counter to the current, all alone and uncaring. (It wasn't even an inch long in the whole open sea, how did I find it?)

Through that mask I saw thousands of things I never could have known were there, and while wearing it I went looking with exactly that in mind.

I saw sleeping sharks swimming in lethargic loops. I saw seaweed knots bulging with life in shafts of sunlight, and the scars on a manatee's shoulders from a jet-ski's impact. I saw tiny shrimps and mammoth reefs, and I sometimes chanced on artefacts from shipwrecks. Not-so-old ones, like the one I almost was. I made some of my best memories of my family and friends through this blue plastic and glass, and it's part of how they remember me. My oldest, best friend's favourite photo is of us in our masks. She keeps it where she'll see it every day.

On a dive, my mask was an aquarium enclosing just my eyes. On dry land, it's a tempered glass pane with potential memories flitting around inside. I suppose they either got in there the same way the sand did, or everything about this mask is a matter of getting what you pay for.

Like I said, my treasure is what you need to find the sunken, hidden, spectacular things. Nowadays, I'm run aground far from my reefs and beaches, and my mask hangs on its own hook next to my keys and umbrella at the front door.

That way I don't forget the value in being able to see without knowing what you'll find.

The Last Post

Franz Grimley

I was driving at the time. It was an unusually bright and sunny day so I had my driver's window wide to the world to enjoy the cooling breeze. All I was really concentrating on was the road ahead when it suddenly, completely out of the blue, smacked me in the head.

No, it wasn't a bee or any other flying insect. It wasn't a solid object at all but I surely felt it just as much as if it had been. It was a smell. It was the smell of newly-cut grass.

The local council was literally making hay while the sun shone and a large tractor-type vehicle was sending up plumes of mown grass as I was passing.

The smell took me instantly to my youth in the small Ayrshire mill town of Darvel. There's a large green play area there called Morton Park and it was always our primary meeting place on a summer's morning before heading off to other areas to spend the day looting and pillaging.

The Park, as we all called it then, in the fifties and sixties, was beautifully maintained, spotlessly clean and a popular destination for trip buses from the Central Belt. As such, the large grassy area which must have encompassed at least a few acres, was never allowed to grow long. Even as a child we could recognise the fact that Mr Scade, the park keeper, was cutting his grass long before we could see him doing it; the smell pervaded the area for, what seemed, miles around.

We learned very quickly that if you squeezed the grass into your hands you had something that resembled a snowball and could spend a good 10 minutes throwing it at each other. It was also very common to run up behind someone, often an unsuspecting girl, and stuff a handful of the clippings down the back of their neck. Such were our early attempts at getting their attention. I'm sure that such activities in that long distant past served to protect us from things like hay fever by giving us a healthy dose of chlorophyll antibodies.

It was this wonderful, fresh smell that triggered my memory and brought me to a place all those long, innocent years before.

A friend and I were lying on the large area of grass that lies at the west end of the park. We'd been playing some game that had involved running around like headless chickens and so I was in resting mode, lying on my back, looking up at the blue sky.

'Did you see my new sodgers?'

My pal Wullie had pulled a couple of toy soldiers from his pocket and began to show me how they were armed and dangerous.

'See, that wan's a sniper. You can tell by the way he's lyin' doon and the way he's pointing his rifle.'

'Is he a German?' I asked, not recognising his uniform.

'Naw, he's a British sodger,' he replied. 'He's a desert rat. You can tell by his khaki shorts.'

At that point I searched in the pockets of my own short trousers (no one wore long trousers or even jeans in those days) and displayed the contents on the grass before us.

I had one lead toy soldier which was missing an arm, four glass marbles, a bit of string, two football cards and a small empty cigar tin that I'd picked up because it looked 'useful'.

'Whit are you gauny dae wae that?' Wullie pointed to the shiny cigar tin.

I opened it to show it was empty and said that I wasn't sure but picking it up seemed a good idea at the time.

58

Then one of us, I can't remember who, suggested we use the tin as a time capsule and bury it under the grass with the express intention of coming back at some point in the future and recovering it.

This was an easy task to accomplish as, in those days, most young boys carried with them a sheath-knife on their belts. I certainly did. As a cub scout we were expected to have such an item and this was long before knives such as these were banned. All it took was a few stern words from your mother about the risks and the dangers and that was enough to frighten you into using it only for the purpose for which it was intended. That's not to say that a friendly game of 'Knifey' was out of the question. But I digress.

I cut out a small square of green turf and laid it aside. I then dug a few inches deeper into the brown loam and scooped it out. Now we were ready for the ceremony.

We then began to fit items into the tin, one each of our soldiers, the football cards and two of the marbles, double-wrapped the tin with the string and, using our hands as trumpets, played the 'Last Post' as we lowered the now sacred tin into the small hole.

I covered it up reverentially with the soil, then plugged the hole with the square of turf. Wullie then saw fit to stamp the plug of turf firmly with his foot. 'There. That'll no come oot noo.'

In order that we'd be able to find the spot again we paced out the distance to the nearest pathway, logged it firmly in our collective memories and promised faithfully to return one day and dig up our buried treasure.

Of course we never did return to dig up our treasure.

Wullie died some time later of some brain related disease or injury. Being a young kid no one ever took the time to explain to me what caused his death. He was just a pal I didn't have any more.

I grew up. Moved away. And life went on.

The hidden treasure was consigned to long-forgotten and dusty memory banks until that day, recently, when someone decided to cut the grass.

Museum of Transport

Mairi Houston

I found my treasure in the old transport museum in Glasgow.

The story that took me there had begun with a tour into my family's history – the little house on the main street in Thornhill where my grandpa, the baker's boy, was born and had slept in the space under the roof; the grander house of my granny, the doctor's daughter; the statue to the exploring ancestor Joseph Thomson, finder of the gazelle; the house at Drumlanrig the family shared with another during the war. Stories, places, names and pictures of people from a past I hadn't known.

Then, a detour into someone else's story. In the churchyard at Keir, incongruous and unassuming – the gravestone of Kirkpatrick Macmillan, the blacksmith's son and, the mossy carved letters proclaimed, 'Inventor of the Bicycle'.

Circuitously, I came to Glasgow, a city I hadn't known, to find out more about the 'Deil on Wheels'. This time, my guide was a boy I'd known when I was a wee girl, all grown up now and working, aptly, I thought, as a cycle courier in the city.

In the Mitchell Library I found news reports on microfiche of Macmillan's 70-mile ride from Cumnock to Glasgow on his new fangled contraption earning him his place in history and a five shilling fine for knocking down an un-named girl in Govan.

From there onto Kelvinside and the object of my quest – the world's first rear wheel propelled bicycle.

And there it was. Behind the camper van, the panda car and the tram and the models of the ships that the men of this city had built. And it was so much less than I'd wanted it to be. It was a contraption that seemed to have been cobbled together from oddments collected in an old man's shed – handles from chisels or bradawls, a garden gate, pedals from an old treadle sewing machine. And that, inglorious, unimpressive, underwhelming, was it· the world's oldest bicycle.

I turned away, ready to brave my disappointment, and instead, I saw it.

My unexpected treasure. A little, scratched and battered, ancient, red and blue tricycle. Not a trike. My trike. The very same. My Tri-ang trike with its sky blue metal box on the back with its cheery perpetually juggling clown. My trike scratched from my scrapes. My box where I'd stored my treasures – my teddy, my rabbit, my dandelion fairies, my dolls, my shells, my pebbles, my jewels, my stories. I am transported.

Here. Not there. Not then. Now. I could touch it if I dared. Right there. I could bring back its cold metal smell. I could grip again its squeaky plastic handlebars and lift the lid and find all my forgotten toys.

I am transfixed. Still. Hand over my mouth to stop whatever this feeling is from coming out and being known. It is a slow motion, sudden, joyful pain.

And in that moment, I look beyond my little trike and see that he sees me. This boy who had known a little of the story of the girl who had fallen from that tricycle. This man now, who, as unexpected as finding my treasure in this place, was, in that very moment, to become my love and the beginning of the next story.

Freedom Machine

Marianne Paget

Part 1

Wheels and Squeals

Clutch yellow handlebars tight. Pump pedals up and down the skinny hall, knees to my ears. Three white wheels spin fast. Make my mouth into a big 'O', puff steam into the cold and I'm Casey Jones on the Cannonball Express. *Woo-woo.* Listen. *Woo-woo*, echoes off canyon walls. Smile – but – Oh no! Cherokees galloping down the mountains. Only way out alive is on horseback. Squeeze my eyes shut, hold my breath and pedal hard as I can to magic the Cannonball Express into... Tonto! Now I am the Lone Ranger. *Yee-ha.*

I just stare at it. Blue bicycle with stabilisers. Try to climb on but it shoogles so I jump off quick. Stabilisers look all wrong. Like Francis in my class with the big shoe and metal on his legs. Francis shoogles when he walks. Want my trike back. Dad laughs. He's been watching me. Says, 'Come on', and opens the front door. Sunshine blazes through, unrolls along the hall floor like Ali Baba's magic carpet right up to my feet, right up to the front wheel of the blue bike. *Wow.* Then I realise – the blue bike is too big for the hall, it has to go outside. Grab the handlebars, puff my chest and march out into the big wide world.

Whheeeeee. Speed. Wind. 'This is fun', I say to Dad, then turn round to see him *not* holding on to the back of my saddle. Heart bangs like a giant drum, then I do see him; way back down the street, grinning, waving.

Bike weaves. Stomach's sick. Head's dizzy. World spins backwards... and I am floating in the Milky Way, watching another me on the blue bike one hundred million miles below, face forward, find balance, take control. Then – blam – I'm in the saddle again, moving fast, noise all around. Hear myself laugh. Hear my dad shout, 'Far enough now'. Grin and pedal on, not looking back.

Part 2

Gears and Years

They pedal over the ridge of the hill, dip out of sight. I take a deep breath to shout after them – then stop. Want them to be safe but want them to grow. Have to trust them, gift them this freedom. Safe enough here in the park surely (although there's the burn and the dogs)? Fold coat tight across my chest. In no time they'll be cycling down to the woods to smoke cigarettes, planning camping weekends with friends, panniers loaded with cheap cider. Then they'll tour Europe, stopping off overlong in Amsterdam's cafes before heading to Greece where they'll trade pedal bikes for motorbikes – no helmets, no leathers, no sense. Scratch scar on my leg with the heel of my opposite foot. Well, it didn't do me too much harm, did it? Flex my weak wrist. Roll it. Shake it. I must have crashed hundreds of times at their age but can only remember the last time. Bouncing along a concrete road leaving layers of skin on tarmac. Limping home weak and shocked. Lifelong love affair with bike in tatters. Press lips together and sigh. Can't avoid it any longer. Will have to shift years of stuff-that-might-come-in-handy to get my bike out of the garage.

Brakes and Stakes

Dust off the frame. Silver scars on black paintwork where it too left its mark on the tarmac. Like me, no real structural damage. Unlike me, no 'trust issues'. Mad to feel betrayed by a bike. Hadn't wanted to keep it, hadn't been able to bring myself to get rid of it. Too much history between us. First bike I'd truly owned. Bought with my own cash. Taken to my own home. Designed it myself, made it what it was. Avoided chic bike boutiques. Found a dark little workshop in a shady Tollcross side street. Artisan mechanic with oil black hands built it to order. Road bike frame; lightweight. Mountain bike handlebars. Shimano gears, 10. And black. Yes, black – please. No other like it. Ran up and downhills with it on my back. Cycled, grimy from days of camping, into glamorous Monte Carlo behind a long-haired blonde in a soft-top red Ferrari. Rolled around country verges with agonizing leg cramps on intercity cycle challenges, trying to keep up with the lads, not drinking enough so I didn't have to pee al fresco in front of them.

Chains and Gains

Straddle it. Take a deep breath. Then step up onto the pedal. Bike wavers forward. The saddle – was it this high before? Will the brakes work? Maybe the chain needs more oil. Want to stop to check but the kids *whoop-whoop* by, on either side, legs like pistons, streets ahead. Need to keep up with them. Need to get moving. Pedal. Breathe. Pedal. Breathe. Soon, shoulders drop. Pedal. Breathe. Fingers loosen around handlebars. Pedal. Breathe. And now I'm 10 years old again, ET in the front basket and we're flying through the air.

Part 3

Life Cycle

Traffic rushes through the city. Blood rushes through my
veins. Riding my bike is a rush: meditation in motion.
It strips away external bluster, silences internal chatter
and directs my focus, lightly, towards balance,
momentum, manoeuvres, logistics. My place in the road.
My place in the great cycle of life.

Smile. Transported, I am free.

Away to the Side
Like Gourock

Kenny Pieper

Amongst the flotsam, a dusty box seemed to be hiding, poking out.

Wiping off the dust and removing the lid, he came across a world long lost to him. The debris of his younger self: concert tickets, football programmes, a birthday card or two. And, long-forgotten, a strange looking piece of plastic. While slightly worn now, the memory remained fresh: and the names scrawled in black pen were unmistakable. A deep breath, a long sigh, the beginnings of a smile...

Four boys run along the beach at Saltcoats. They were there on a council run bus trip. It was the summer holidays and the predictability of the destination had long taken the mystery out of 'Mystery Tour'. Four boys. Saltcoats beach. Nothing to do. Sandwiches eaten before they had left East Kilbride. The little money they had, spent on fruit machines and video games. But they are boys and they are never bored. Coins chipped in for a ball, a plastic ball for a quick game on the beach. A light ball. It's plastic. This is Saltcoats. Windy wouldn't do it justice.

With hours to go they begin a game of kicking the ball into the sea to see how far it will travel. And it travels.

And travels.

They follow it for miles. It almost comes back to shore, teases them, never quite gets there. But they persist as boys of that age do. They arc together and that is important to them; they would not be anywhere else than here; together.

Eventually they catch it. They have come so far.

A bus to catch home, a memory to share. A penknife is produced, a pen. Sharing everything as friends do. Along with the memory they would all take a little piece of that day with them. Shared equally.

A joyful reminder in a dusty box. One day they may fit all of the pieces together. Perhaps. But a long forgotten day by the seaside will remain forever. The plastic is returned, more valuable than before, the box returned to its rightful place. But the smile stays.

The smile stays.

The Ball

Iain Reynolds

Well, if you got as far as reading this, then you will have noticed that the photo is of a ball: a marbled-effect, sponge ball. It's about four inches in diameter. I must have first held it when I was about one or two years old. Though I don't remember holding it until I was about five. It was to be found, sitting on the mantelpiece and prevented from rolling off it by a shallow, brown plastic dish, which, it was revealed later in life, was used to stop the castors on the couch making indentations on the nice carpet. The wee dish, when turned upside down, looked a dead-ringer for a chocolate yo-yo biscuit, and was often paraded as such by older brothers. The ball lived at Gran and Grandpa's house in Ravenswood, Cumbernauld.

When we went there, there was not a lot to play with. There were binoculars, which my brothers and I used to peer across the A80, to the fields in what is now the sprawl of Dullatur and Balloch. And, there was the ball. It always started the day on the mantelpiece, and always had to be put there afterwards, in the wee dish. Not putting it in the dish and watching the ball slowly roll off onto the wooden hearth was not appreciated by Gran. Though, I am sure Grandpa liked to see us trying it on.

Anyone who has lived in or walked around Cumbernauld will know the cobbled up-stands which fringe the pavements. These were great for bouncing the ball off, for hours. Being built on the side of a hill, Ravenswood was not the ideal place to leave a ball unattended. Even a minute's lapse of concentration could see the ball snake its way off for blocks and blocks.

In 1998, 10 years after my grandpa, my gran passed away. All the grandkids were now in their late teens and 20s and all had a part to play in the emptying of the house. I like to think that everyone got a memento of life in that house. But, it was the wee ball which had meant the most to me. When we visited the house, before the funeral, I was on it like a hawk. It probably never even featured on anyone else's radar, so quickly was it stuffed into my pocket.

From then on, wherever I went travelling, the ball went with me. A year or so later, when living in the States, I was at a barbeque with my workmates and we had the ball out, playing catch in a field of long wheat. It was idyllic and is, to this day, one of the most memorable, yet simple days I had in my time in America. I remember dreaming, as we hurled the ball, of all the different nationalities that were in the game, and the fact that they were playing with a wee ball I had always known. Then, one wayward throw, and it was gone, lost in the long grass. The more we looked for it, the more we simply trampled the grass and made it harder to find. I was gutted. One other guy, Ben, stayed with me for a while looking for it while the rest, quite understandably, headed back to the barbeque and the beers.

After about half an hour, I gave up and collected my thoughts and felt sad to have lost it, yet quite chuffed at 'where' I had lost it and how it had been lost. A full hour later, I felt Ben staring at me, menacingly, and turned round to find him animatedly trying to get his chops around this huge burger bun, with the ball inside it. 'You, brilliant, brilliant bastard', I shouted, 'when the hell did you find that?' I shrieked. Ben had found it after about 20 minutes and, knowing its meaning to me, was just intrigued as to how long I would stay looking. This did nothing but reinforce the worth of the ball to me.

My story ends in 2005, with my now wife, Annie and I heading off back-packing around the world. With only a rucksack to carry all our worldly goods for what turned out to be 30 months; of course, the ball came with me. Six months into our trip and in the Argentinian town of Salta, we stopped in at a brilliant ramshackle hostel. We sat for hours chatting with fellow travellers, while the resident Jack Russell dog played with the ball. Annie and I headed out to get some food, while I thought nothing of leaving the dog to play with the ball. The ball never rolled again, as when we arrived back, the dog had chewed the ball into more pieces than I care to dwell on. It was gone. Not lost, but ruined. I laugh about it now, but I never thought that I would have lost the ball in such a crap, unsatisfying way. And for days after, I cursed the fact that, to my knowledge, I had not even a photo featuring the wee thing.

And here stands the case for taking pictures of the things that mean so much to you, regardless of how constant or commonplace they may seem. I found my treasure about three years after that ball was eaten, when flicking through some old photos of years past. On the night of the barbeque, at which I had temporarily 'lost' the ball, I had, drunkenly, decided to take a close-up photo of it on my bedsheet. And now it's all I have to help me reminisce of the many hours and the many hands which helped this ball fly through the air.

Recorded memories

Garden of Birds

Richard Holloway

She was on the run from an abusive partner when she
moved in with us. After all, we had plenty of room.
The rectory was a tall baronial house with a crow-
stepped gable and a conical roof turret. Set in the
middle of a row of 19th-century tenements in the
coldest street in Edinburgh, we loved every refrigerated
room of the place and filled it with curates and students
and people in trouble. We gave her a room in the attic,
looking out over Waverley Station to the Governor's
Palace of the old city prison on Calton Hill and the
windowed cliff at the back of Saint Andrew's House.
She loved the room and we loved having her to stay –
for as long as she needed, we told her.

One day she came to me. She felt bad about paying
no rent, though she had no money to pay it with: was
there some way she could contribute? You're an artist,
I said, make us a picture. Paint your rent. That'll do.
She was indeed an artist. She painted miniatures, tiny
works of finely detailed art, often done with what
looked to me like a single hair. It will be lovely to have a
tiny painting from her, I thought, maybe of a greenfinch.
She knew I loved greenfinches.

Months later she invited us to view the painting.
I was surprised she didn't bring it down to the kitchen,
the room around which the life of the house revolved.
But up the stairs we went, right under the conical roof
turret of the old house, into her room. And there in the
corner under a cloth was an enormous rectangular
shaped object. Shyly, she pulled the cloth aside and
revealed the massive painting, which had to be six feet

high by four feet broad. Yet it was undoubtedly a miniature, a gigantic miniature! At the top of the painting there was a range of lavender coloured mountains, but in the foreground there was a walled garden, a Persian garden, with a lily pond and a large mystical tree alive with butterflies. And there were birds everywhere, 43 of them. Some of them were deadly serious, such as the two secretary birds walking purposefully along the wall of the pond like a couple of Edinburgh advocates going up the Mound to try a case in the High Court. Some of them were comical. One seemed to be parachuting into the garden, legs splayed and an embarrassed look on his face. I couldn't find a greenfinch, but there was proud looking bullfinch and a large barn owl with wide amazed eyes.

And all three of our children were in the painting! Annie, our eldest, was sitting on a coloured blanket, surrounded by a flurry of birds pecking seeds from the open palm of her right hand. There was Sara, our middle child, further up the picture on the left, holding a large hawk in her arms. And they were wearing dresses their mother had made for them, perfectly captured to the last detail, Annie's in her favourite pink, Sara's in a warm brown corduroy. Mark, our youngest, was there too, floating blissfully in the lily pond, tickling his toe with a feather!

We were overwhelmed. This was not rent! This was a supreme work of art to cherish all our days. And in every house we've lived in since the day of its unveiling, it has had pride of place. The artist found love again and moved away, but never from our lives, never from our hearts. Our children grew up and left home, one of them very far away, and became middle-aged as we became old. Yet there they are, children still in that garden of birds on the wall of our sitting room. The painting will outlive us and will have to find a home with our children when we are gone. It will outlive them as well, and when they die go somewhere else – we know not where – because humans depart but art abides. Maybe one day it will find a permanent home in a Scottish gallery and years hence people will wonder who they were, those children, and how they came to find themselves in that garden. And the rent will go on being paid.

World Service

Hardeep Singh Kohli

Is she still waiting for the news or has she already received it? Are her sorry shoulders slouched with aching anticipation or is her soul shattered by an announcement, already arrived? Is the radio resonating reports or has it been hastily, heedlessly hushed? 'World Service'.

East Kilbride. I had cousins that lived in East Kilbride. I spent a great deal of the 1980s on the pathways in the precincts of East Kilbride. EK (as we affectionately referred to the town planners' homage to concrete) has punched above its weight in gifting the wider world greatness. Songsmith *par excellence* Roddy Frame from Aztec Camera; George Orwell himself wrote tracts of *1984* whilst being treated for TB in Hairmyres Hospital; and *Balamory*'s iconic Miss Hoolie (aka Julie Nimmo) calls EK 'hame'. Add one more name to that list: enigmatic artist Anthony Scullion.

Scullion is a graduate of the Glasgow School of Art, an internationally renowned, incredible institute that for decades has defined the very quintessence of the Scottish soul when it comes to creative expression. The Art School, like EK, has a special place in my life. My Jesuit secondary school was across the road from the uber-hip Art School. Scott Street to the west, Dalhousie to the east; I doubt there were two more unlikely institutes of education so closely combined.

I've never met Tony Scullion. That fact is rather strange since he has impacted on my life in a peerless and profound way. His painting 'World Service' is unarguably my favourite painting in the world. I happened upon it some years back after my marriage melted messily into a myriad of memories. I found myself alone; and I found Anthony Scullion.

Like all the best art, 'World Service' asks more questions than it offers answers. The solitude, the vast, barely inhabited canvas seemed to mirror my own life at the time. And yet for all its enigma, for the chasm of unanswered questions there is a feast of familiarity. My ex-wife's uncle had a radio repair shop in Bombay and he gifted me a radio very much like the one in the painting. An old university classmate from law school introduced me to the piece. I believe it was painted in a neighbourhood I had once lived in. Apart from all of that, radio broadcasting is at the very heart of my life. So many strands; somehow drawn together. 'World Service'.

We weren't the sort of family that grew up surrounded by art. My parents were immigrants, more interested in feeding, housing and educating their progeny; the arts were an indulgence, not for the likes of us. Besides, what practical use were paintings, theatre and dance? Luckily Meadowburn Primary School took eight-year-old Hardeep and my class to Kelvingrove Art Gallery. I'd never been to an art gallery in my life; I doubt I'd even heard the word gallery spoken in my house.

I'll never forget seeing Dali's 'Christ of St John of the Cross'. That day in 1975 changed my life; forever. The next time a politician talks about decimating the arts budgets further still, closing yet more libraries or allowing a beloved painting to leave the country, imagine the Hardeep that never saw Dali's surrealist masterpiece, Hardeep the chartered accountant. That Hardeep never learnt what it was to celebrate the senses or be elevated by art. (Having said that, he's pretty good with an Excel spreadsheet.)

'World Service'. Shoeless, coat on, her back to the light, it would be easy to feel just despondency, the aching emptiness of this painting. But I don't. The sparseness speaks to the spirit. Scullion somehow scrutinises the substance the soul. Like the bittersweet beauty of Justin Currie; the insightful intelligence of Muriel Spark; the elegant ebullience of Bill Forsyth, Anthony Scullion held out a hand to me and I happily held it. He helped me through a difficult and challenging part of my life. 'World Service' served my world; it's a painting I will forever treasure.

Grandma's Book of Poems

Udita Banerjee

A plain brown cover, stitched onto a book… handbound with great care. Yellow pages, black words, blue ink – quite the palette.

My grandma's book of poetry from her classes of English Literature at Calcutta University is a testimony.

It is a memory of a simpler time when books were companions, dressed up or down with needle and thread by hands that sewed with as much dexterity as they wrote.

A testimony of Grandma's thoughts on Shakespeare and Tennyson, on Milton and Yeats. Not scribbled hastily, but written in curling cursive along a margin with a fountain pen. A diligent, honest attempt at understanding a foreign language, a faraway culture, and its people from their verse… a simple understanding of words with words, a dialogue of greats.

Saree clad, with kohl in her eyes and flowers in her hair, Grandma was no Lucy Gray. But in the pages of a book lies the promise of a lifetime of romance with books and words – a love Dida passed on to her daughter – my ma, and she, to me – a promise that still holds strong every time I see them.

Her eyes give her trouble now, her ears aren't as sharp either, hands tremble ever so slightly as she puts words down to paper – life has not brought her to Britain yet – but the intellect is still razor edged.

A conversation with Wordsworth and Keats, Byron and Shelley are incomplete without Grandma's notes on the margin, in blue, on yellow pages, in the brown treasure trove.

Her Yard No. is 867

Melvin Barnes

Her yard no. is 867: she has a gross weight of 5034 tons; is 370 feet long; 53 feet wide, with a depth of 28 feet. Built by the Hall Russell Group, Aberdeen, for the Burnett Steamship Company, she is the motor vessel *Holmside*. She is berthed alongside the hall telephone and is dusted frequently.

Designed with a weather eye on the navigation of the new St Lawrence Seaway; she carried cargo for Burnett's for 10 years, until being sold and renamed MV *Cabinda* in 1969. During the seventies, she continued to ply the oceans as a bulk sugar/ore/grain carrier. Sadly, the vessel's last entry in Lloyds Register is in 1981–82, and notes that MV *Cabinda* had been wrecked at Casablanca.

In the real world, the world of physical things, sadly, both MV *Holmside*, and her alter ego have gone. In the world of dreams and memories, however, that is quite a different matter. Captured by a photographer on the day of her launch; she remains forever, punching her way through the choppy waters of the North Sea, before turning westwards to ply her trade on the other side of the Atlantic.

Holmside, launched on the 21st of May 1959, is more than just a blending of light-sensitive chemicals, and glossy paper; suspended in time. She is more than just an image in black and white surrounded by a wooden frame; this is not just a photograph. It is, simultaneously, a personal treasure, and a portal to the past.

When I joined her at Newcastle in 1960, I was 17 years old. In that year, *Holmside* headed for Cornwall (Fowey) to pick up a cargo of china clay to be delivered to Montreal; the beginning of a voyage that would last a year; taking in Canada, the St Lawrence Seaway, the Welland canal, and the great lakes of the Unites States of America. It may have been a long time ago, but I can still hear the deep thrum of the Sulzer diesel engines as she headed up the St Lawrence River to a berth just south of the Jacques Cartier Bridge: I could barely wait to go ashore.

I remember watching impatiently 'till the gangway between the ship and the shore was lowered. Even then, I had to wait while ship chandlers and dockworkers came aboard to assist in the decanting of the ship's cargo. Eventually it was my turn; I practically ran across the gangway. I made my way out of the dock area to the edge of the city: St Catherine's Street. I stood by the side of the road, and watched the constant flow of cars, wondering if I could cross, without being run over. Most of the cars seemed to be twice the length of cars in Scotland. More than a few had swept wings at the rear: they looked like something out of a science fiction film: I found out later, they were Chevrolets.

I will never forget my first conversation with someone from another country. Wishing to buy postcards to send home, I found myself in the Seaman's Mission. Now, due no doubt to my accent, and my evident youth, the man behind the shop's counter asked me where I was from, and how old I was. 'Scotland,' I replied, 'and I'm 18 in October.' (Why, when we're young, do we add a year on?) He then asked me, and I don't know why, 'Do you have a car?'

I told him I didn't. Crivens, I didn't even own a pushbike. 'Really?' was the reply. 'My grandson, who's 18, has a car, a swimming pool, and a dog.' What each had to do with the other, I knoweth not what: I did not press the matter further.

'Have a nice day,' he said, and I went looking for somewhere to write out post cards and lick stamps.

Today, *Holmside* sits in the company of other images, subtly reminding us of the inexorable passage of time. She is different, of course, from the family and school group photographs. She is personal. After all, in this house, I am the only one to have set foot upon her deck. When I look at her image, I see the colour of the after-deck guard railings; I feel the steps of the after-companionway as I descend to the crews' accommodation; I feel the key in my hand. I turn the key in the lock. I open the door. I walk into the cabin and see the gleaming brass portholes, the clothes lockers, the writing desk, and the bunk that I lay in when off duty. I am the thief of time, and 17 once more.

VHS Tape:
Christening 1984

Peggy Hughes

Here comes my grandfather, football legend Sammy
Hughes (1926–2011), through the front door. He lifts
my big three-year-old brother up by the oxters, straight
into the air and laughs – 'Ho what happened to you
boy? Where did ye disappear off to?' A reedy wee voice
– my five-year-old brother off camera – pipes up: 'Ryan
was a bad boy, Granda. He climbed on the [communion!]
table. Aunt Pat had to bring him home in the middle!
Granny said I was like a wee king but...' We're
immediately into the action of a Sunday in February,
early afternoon in a small house in the north-east of
Northern Ireland. Now Great Aunt Maureen, our elder
stateswoman, famous for being able to start a row in an
empty house and finish it too, fills the doorway. Her
sister, my grandmother Elizabeth, follows. At full fleet,
these women of the Cameron Clan are Mitfordesque, in
number, in glamour. 'Smile Lizzie, you're on candid
camera!' The wonderful Elizabeth famously hates having
her photo taken and jigs out of the road. At 86 she still
has a sharp word for everyone, still hates having her
photo taken. It's our old house (hasn't been ours since
1996), those 'oul' curtains, that memorable wallpaper,
people arriving and noise.

In the living room Uncle Alan is doing his Donald
Duck impression (he's still got it!) and, lone Spurs
supporter, is slagging off Man. United. My brothers are
following the camera between rooms: too small to be
visible, but perfectly audible. The biggest wants his hair

combed, the smaller is intoning again and again to everyone and no one at once: 'this is how it works'. A toy helicopter, apparently. I'm being fussed over in a gown, a small, unknowable meringue, in my lovely mother's arms. All hail the first (and only) granddaughter in the Hughes line! I'm being awful good. Amn't I? Auch look! Was that a wee smile? Give us a wee smile! Tell us a story! Ah she's tired. In the kitchen and behold the late, great Pearl, my paternal grandmother: not a hair out of place, the best silk blouse in the business, and I'd bet you a tenner that's a vodka and brown lemonade in that glass. She bounces my brother on her knee and tells him a serious wee rhyme about cherry blossoms. Sausage rolls and sandwiches and a pink and white cake are on the sideboard. The impromptu bar is raring to go.

The year is 1984, the occasion my christening. The cameraman and narrator is my da; he is 29 (my age now) and though he doesn't appear in the video, I can tell you from photographic evidence and legend that he is in his experimental and short-lived moustache phase and wearing his good brown three-piece suit with a fat tie. He has borrowed this vast piece of camera kit from a pal especially for today. The camera was, I'm told, worn on the back like Egon Spengler's Proton Pack and weighed a ton.

Many of this incomparable cast are no longer with us. Or they are with us in memory, if not in person. My brothers, never mind my parents, have grey hair now! Mine is getting there too! Here is the universe and such hope and cheer in one room, on one ancient-seeming eighties afternoon. Aunt Jacqueline, Uncle Bob, Great Uncle Jim, Jimmy Clarke, is that Glen? Cousins, neighbours, friends! There they are, they're all here. This tired, treasured old VHS is a time machine.

A blockbuster, a crowd-pleaser and a trip down memory lane: a thing so special that many miles and moons away, from a different town on the north-east of a different country, it brings a lump to my throat just watching it in my head.

The Resonant Chord

Gill Monaghan

Of all the things I've ever lost, it's still the one thing I miss the most... I remember the day the padded A4 envelope with the Manchester postmark landed through the letterbox. Its contents: one six-page A4 lined letter, one cartoonish doodle of the author, a Cadbury's Boost and... a tape. Grinning from ear to ear, I hurriedly crossed the room, opened the deck on my stereo system and slid the Sony C90 into it. Then I pressed play and waited, laughing as I noted the title of the compilation, 'S'all Gravy'.

Opening the clear case, I lifted the inlay out and read the intricately scribed track-listing as the music played in the background. That first track was by Cold Cut and it was called 'Atomic Moog'. It was out-of-this-world genius. It was followed by tracks by Tiger, Pulp, Hefner, Bis, The Fall, One Dove, DJ Shadow, The Doors, Yummy Fur, Ash, Kenickie, Elastica, The Chemical Brothers, Spare Snare and The Smiths. Interspersed amongst these were a few spoken word interludes, one by John Cooper Clarke which made me laugh, another was from DJ Shadow's 'Endtroducing' album. It was, quite simply, THE best compilation tape ever made and I played it to death at every available opportunity – so much so that I feared it might snap! It was the soundtrack to many a morning pottering around getting ready for the day ahead, many an evening getting ready to go out with friends and many a late-nighter procrastinating over an essay. It even sound-tracked the walk up to university most mornings, such was its aural brilliance. I quickly returned the gesture with a compilation entitled 'The Difficult 2nd Album' of which, I received plaudits for... and thus, a friendship was born.

Michael and I were each other's musical stem cells. Just when one of us thought that they'd heard everything and that our musical knowledge was saturated, another C90 would thud through our letter boxes, its contents filled with whole, new harmonious – and sometimes discordant – worlds. We knew how to tickle each others' funny bones as well as flex our musical muscles from 170 miles apart. A typical letter would commence with an update of The Time, The Place, and the all-important S.O.M (state of mind): example 'Ninja-sharp but fluffy' or 'Tip top and degenerate', as well as this week's 'heroes and villains' list. Example: Heroes – Jarvis Cocker for mooning at the Brits, buy-one-get-one-free offers and Converse trainers and Villains – Tony Blair (a politician, of whom, we agreed *should* have been channelling his energies into reforming his garage rock band), single re-releases, designer stubble and rocket leaves in sandwiches. We would always sign off with some finely-tuned witticism or other such as 'Stay safe, stay warm and remember to claim your winter heating allowance!' or 'Godspeed young slayer of virtue!'

I had just sent him what I considered to be, my finest work yet, a compilation of torch songs by the likes of Billie Holiday, Bobbie Gentry, Nick Cave and Scott Walker sings Brel, and had waited the usual couple of days for a typical response and review... but no dice. One month later and he finally got back to me. He had met a girl called Helen and he had fallen in love. He sounded happy and I was pleased for him. I mean, you can't stay cooped up in your student gaff making up compilation tapes and writing to a girl from miles away forever now can you? The letters to-and-fro became less frequent but the banter was still magnificent – until one day... nothing... and then... still nothing. It was strange but around that same time, 'S'All Gravy: THE Best Compilation in the World' disappeared... just vanished one day, without a trace. This was the holy cow of compilations. My musical zenith. I was gutted. It was the thing that had kick-started and cemented a long-distance friendship and now, its disappearance was the thing that represented the end of that.

Of all the things I've ever lost, it's still the one thing I miss the most... and yeah, the tape was brilliant too.

All of Us Are Still Alive

Martin Stepek

18 August 1940

Oh my dearest!

We received your letter of 7 July luckily. All of us are still alive. There are now lots of berries and mushrooms so we're eating them and some we're selling. Somehow we're managing but what will winter make of us? Will we still be alive after that? All of us are barefoot and the winter lasts eight months and starts in two months' time. I don't know how we'll cope with that. We're missing everyone but life has to go on.

I could write quite a lot but we can't write about some things. It's such a good thing you know where we are. Henrik and his family were taken to Russia as well. We don't have any news of them. Gutek Konopnicki is in Russia too. Irena is in Lwow. She is having to get through her tragedy alone. Please don't forget about us and try to get us out of here. Send my love to Cziek's family.

Janina

I sometimes try to imagine receiving this letter. Your wife and your three teenage children have been taken from your home in your absence, and sent by cattle truck to a Soviet labour camp at the edge of the Arctic Circle.

The man who received this letter, my grandfather Wladyslaw, had evaded execution by the Red Army and at the time he receives this letter is in hiding from the Nazis. He is in the Polish resistance. The great world issues whirl around him: the fight for democracy against fascism and communism; the giant figures who symbolise these ideologies – Hitler, Churchill, Stalin; the slaughter of Poland's Jewish population whom he had advised on land issues, the mass enslavement and murder of his fellow Poles. It is the second time in barely 20 years he has had to fight for his country's freedom, having led a local insurrection at the end of the First World War.

But now he has confirmation that his wife Janina and his three children are still alive. What do war, power struggles, grand ideologies matter when your 12-year-old daughter is barefoot in the Soviet GULAG? She had just finished primary school for God's sake.

This letter is my connection with the grandparents I never knew, and with the lost way of life for the 30 million citizens who lived in the Polish Second Republic of 1918–1939. Wladyslaw and Janina were not to be reunited. Janina was never to set foot on Polish soil again. She and her three children – my father Jan and his two sisters Zosia and Danka – were released a year after she wrote this letter and made their way south through Russia, eventually reaching Persia in the summer of 1942. But it was too late for Janina. She died of starvation in a hospital in Teheran on 25th October 1942. My father was 20 at the time, recovering from typhus, still fighting dysentery and malaria. He could put his hand round his thigh and touch his finger and thumb. Zosia was sick from a series of illnesses and Danka weighed 3 stone 12 pounds. She was 15.

How do you begin to understand this? Hundreds of thousands of their fellow Poles deported to Russia died there. Their graves are spread through every part of the massive Soviet landmass. Unnamed, unmarked, unvisited. My family are lucky. Janina has a headstone, even though the neat cemetery in Teheran in which she is buried masks a colder reality. Underneath the gravestones are mass graves with lines of coffins laid out beside each other. The names on the headstones bear no relationship to precisely where in the cemetery each body is buried. But at least we know Janina lies somewhere there. Much of the vast Polish diaspora scattered around the world after the Second World War can never find out where their parents, siblings, grandparents lie in the unimaginable vastness of what was the Soviet Union.

Pre war Poland was a remarkable but volatile mix of Poles, Ukrainians, Jews, Germans and other minorities. The dream of regaining independence in 1918 turned into the nightmare of the Holocaust in which almost all of Poland's three million Jews perished. The same number of ethnic Poles were murdered or starved. Warsaw was completely destroyed by the Nazis. Stalin annexed the eastern half of the country. The post-war communists expelled the entire German Polish population, and over a million Poles were forcibly relocated to new lands taken from Germany. Wartime resistance leaders were executed after the war by Stalin's secret police. All this in just six years. Poland was then subjected to 45 years of communist dictatorship under Soviet command. Only in 1989 did Poland finally emerge from the direct consequences of the Second World War. It will take generations for the country to fully come to terms with what happened to it.

The epic tragedy of multi-cultural pre-war Poland is a country that is now scarred by death camps from Nazi occupation, the still unhealed heartbreak of the Holocaust, the Katyn massacres, the little-reported shooting of children in reprisal for their parents committing the crime of helping a Jew. All of this pours out when I hold the letter my grandmother wrote to her husband in 1940.

But it reduces to this. I never knew her. Nor him. I was not to be Polish, but Scottish. I was never to play in the family farm's fields of corn, never to skip school or church in order to pick blueberries in the fertile soil of beautiful Haczow, where Wladyslaw lies buried. He had died of cancer in 1943 unaware that his children had escaped to freedom.

This letter awakens my private world of deepest love and grief for two people I never knew, of an alternate life unlived. It opens up a universe of inhumanity I can scarcely imagine. This is my heritage. I don't seek to understand it, just to feel it.

Found objects

Smells Like Bat Table

Ewan Morrison

Picture this – Bat Woman and the ghost of Kurt Cobain hobbling down the street under the weight of a vintage, rustic oak leaf table. They stop every 10 feet or so for breath and to re-adjust their hold (as the table is heavy even for a superhero), trying not to meet the eye of bemused passers-by. After a pause to regain energy, they nod to each other from across its length (Bat Woman re-adjusting her mask and Cobain taking a deep breath) then they bend at the knees and hoist it back up again and toddle down a steep hill; its oak leaves flap back and forward, bashing fingers and extracting curses from both Bat Woman and the ghost of the deceased American musician who rose to fame with the album 'Nevermind'.

This actually happened.

Oh yes, and please picture this event in dour, grey Glasgow, a place not well known for its superheroes – although arguably it has plenty of ghosts.

It should also be said that I, personally, was the ghost of Kurt Cobain and my wife was Bat Woman and that it was Halloween.

First of all – the table. Like many couples of the arty-beatniky variety, my wife and I have a problem with the generic nature of modern commodities. We've been to the other side of the world and discovered friends with the same Ikea Lillehammer beds and the same shelving units that Ikea named 'Lack'. Such furniture is there to remind us that we are all the same, not in the socialist sense but in the horrible banality of global consumerism. Denying this trend though creates a problem – either you just throw in the towel and go to Ikea when you need a kitchen table, or you do as we did and spend month after month trawling round charity shops and antique shops looking for The One – that great authentic one-of-a-kind table (or for that matter toilet bowl, or sink or rug) that will prove that you are not a machine-made reproduction of a person, but a unique, possibly antique, individual. It is nearly an impossible task, because essentially what we were doing was looking for lost treasure.

Digression: there is a also a 'law of diminishing returns' at work here, historically, as even secondhand shops are now filling up with Ikea, and there is an increasing lack of genuine antiques – one day Ikea will in fact be the only antiques left. We shall be in a world of Lack.

Back to Kurt Cobain and Bat Woman.

So, in the weeks before Halloween, the-wife-who-would-soon-be-Bat Woman and I had got very grumpy with each other over our failure to find a dining room table. 'For God sake, how much longer do we have to eat our food off our knees?', 'Can't we just admit defeat and go to Ikea?' This is the kind of small quibbling detail that can lead to major marital rifts. When a man says to his wife 'Can't we just go to Ikea?' what he is really saying is that he considers his marriage fairly generic and nothing special – he might as well say 'I'm making do with you even though I could get someone just like you off the shelf'. Wives tend not to find this flattering.

So it was on the Halloween in question that such an argument had just occurred. I was in the wrong, which might explain why I had decided to dress up as the ghost of Cobain, effectively the ghost of a failure, and there may have been some animosity towards women in my choosing to write 'Courtney Did It' on my torn T-shirt in fake blood. The fact that my wife felt the need to dress as a superhero may also have had some hidden significance.

So, costumed and rather foul-of-mood after yet another meal, eaten from our laps, while staring into the empty space where a table should be, we decided that we'd have to 'bite the bullet' and the very next day venture to the accursed big blue shed to buy conformist furniture. We were also a little depressed about how our costumes were maybe a bit try-hard and childish for two grown-ups. Maybe it was time for us to really be mature and give up the infantile idea that we were special unique people.

The time came and we had to walk over several hills in the cold and dark to pick up the kids, when lo and behold (or as Bat Woman might say KA-POWW!) there it was: This extremely buggered-up, scratched, muddy, vintage double-leaf table, sitting among some scraps of flooring and bin bags, which some new home owner had put out for the council sanitation workers to take away the next day.

What would you do? We debated the possibility of coming back to get it the next day, with the car, when we weren't dressed as a superhero and a ghost. But Bat Woman decreed that this was an absolute treasure and that although it wasn't really possible to see the quality and texture of the wood in the dull street lights, surely, if we walked past it for even a minute, someone else would come and steal it.

So we decided, there and then, to postpone our festivities and lug the table back to our table-less abode.

Years later, we still have the damn thing. It's a pain in the ass. People's fingers are always getting jammed in the leaves. Our legs bash off its legs all the time. It's wobbly. Bleaching the dirt off its legs only added more stains. We gave up trying to scrape back the layers of paint still remaining around its edges – which was probably the reason it was thrown out in the first place and God knows how many previous owners had also given up on trying to 'restore' it. But we value it highly – this is not just because it cost us nothing but because, as Friedrich Nietzsche (the father of all superheroes) once said: 'A thing does not have value unless it is won through a struggle.' Also there is something to be said for finding beauty among other people's crap.

As Kurt Cobain once sang 'Come, Dowsed in mud, Soaked in bleach, As I want you to be, As a trend, As a friend. As an old memory.'

We love our messy, scratchy, scratched unstable table and think the real Kurt Cobain (Bat Woman, we're not so sure about) would have loved it too. Everyone asks us 'Where the hell did you find that thing?' and that, best of all, gives us a story to tell, which is something Ikea can never offer.

The Toffee Stone

Maureen Black

I was brought up in a mining town in Midlothian and my dad worked down the pit all his life. Therefore he made the most of being outside in the fresh air.

Every Saturday he and I used to go for a long walk – winter, summer, wet or dry, we would leave the house just after lunch and trek up the hill to Somerville's Farm and along to Fordel. At Fordel we would stop and my dad would go into the shop and buy a small bar of Highland Toffee. (This was a special Saturday treat.) Then we would walk together to a small layby at the side of the road where there was a big wooden bench. Dad would sit on the bench and it was my job to go looking around in the grass and bushes to find our special 'toffee stone'. Each week I would bring several stones back one at a time and we would look at each one together and decide if it was the 'right' toffee stone. I would have to search for quite a while and find quite a few stones before suddenly my dad would say 'that's it, that's the one'. That signalled the beginning of the toffee ceremony.

The toffee would be carefully unwrapped and placed in a big, clean, cotton hanky to make sure we didn't lose any toffee. A decision then had to be made as to the best place to tap the toffee to make sure it broke into lots of small pieces. The first piece had to be carefully chosen. Not too big and not too small and I can still remember that creamy taste as it melted on my tongue. We would then sit cuddled up together, me savouring the toffee, whilst my dad would be telling me stories about cows that could talk and sheep that could dance, using the nature around us to inspire wonderful tales.

Before we left it was important to ensure the toffee stone was well hidden away again so it could be found and used again the following week. Unfortunately the fairies always seemed to move it during the week (they were always hoping to find a piece of toffee so my dad said). No matter how safely it was hidden it never seemed to be in the same place the next week.

When I was older and had my own children I took them to the layby with a bar of Highland Toffee and told them the story and we looked for our own toffee stone. This I have kept and perhaps one day I will go with my grandchildren and tell them the story and break toffee with my grandchildren.

Even today when I see or eat toffee I am reminded of my dad and the toffee stone.

Birthstone

Elaine Marie McKay

Part of a 19-storey building sits on my window ledge – a 'chip off the old block' of high rise flats where I was born and raised. I am not sure which part of the building it is from. It might be from the backstairs I was forbidden to go near as a kid (part of me hopes so). It might be from the very room in which I was born (unlikely given that in one block there were 114 living spaces or spaces for living i.e. the gaps between towering concrete).

How did I get it? My third child was born and the building newly demolished. My husband threw away the bunches of clichés and came to the visiting hour with a boulder in a plastic bag. He looked nervous but pleased. The gift was prefaced, 'I hope you like this. I know it's not the usual type of thing, but I thought you'd appreciate it!' He had gone to the crumpled building that used to be home. Slipping past the bored security guard, he had salvaged a grey piece of concrete from the pile of rubble. Just for me and I got it!

I held the ugly pockmarked boulder in my hand and felt the romance and the love. Love not only for my husband, but for my mother who had brought me into the world nine storeys up into the air, but who hadn't lived long enough to see any of my beautiful kids. It brought together my own birth, the birth of my son and the woman who never got to visit me in a maternity ward, and whom I so desperately missed.

I also knew my affection for this rock was ironic. The buildings themselves were ugly beasts that families were jammed into by the dozen. (If we saw further than others, it was by standing on the shoulders of the family downstairs.) There were no aesthetics; just tiles and fire-escape verandas. Cathkin Braes was our wild and communal garden.

However, I felt nostalgic for my childhood every time I had driven past those five Mitchellhill Giants and nostalgic for the kids who grew up alongside me, and up above me, and down below me. Not only did you know people's names but the number of the landing they lived on became part of their identity too:

'The so-and-sos. They live up on 10.'

'Such-and-such on 6.'

I have no idea from what storey my concrete piece was flung. It sits varnished now, on my window ledge, still ugly but my treasure, just the same.

Cowries

Flora Napier

As a wee girl in the seventies I spent most of my summer holidays in Dornoch, where my grandparents lived. My siblings and I loved the town (actually a cathedral city), with its wide high street, home to the weekly pipe band practice on a Saturday night and lined with touristy shops; the fields surrounding my grandfather's house, where we took a neighbour's dog for walks and watched it hopelessly chase rabbits; and the sunny walled garden and orchard where my grandfather patiently grafted fruit trees, a hobby he had picked up living and working as a doctor in Peru. More than anything we loved the endless, white sandy beaches that stretched up and down the coast for miles in either direction.

Every year we would race to the beach at the earliest opportunity, stopping only to select an array of brashly coloured buckets and spades from the local shops (transformed into Aladdin's caves of tourist tat over the summer months). Once we had arrived, passing the golf course clubhouse and the caravan site on the right and miles of scratchy machair-covered dunes to the left, we would inspect the panorama; comparing what lay before us with memories from previous visits. Here was the best place to pitch camp for the day, with the obligatory stripy wind-breaker, rugs and picnic bag; there was the huge rock from which you could dive into the sea when the tide was fully in (or lose a shoe to an unexpectedly big wave, the other shoe later being donated to the neighbour's grateful dog); and there, further on, the best rock-pooling spot.

After an hour or so of splashing and exploring, one

of us three would plonk down on the sand and begin the annual serious business of cowrie-hunting.

'Cowrie' is the name given to a particular type of seashell found washed up on beaches. Further north (I've since been informed by lots of folk) they're called 'Groatie buckies'. Tiny, pinky-white and delicate-looking (but actually rock hard), the shells are a softened oval, ribbed with curved lines. They look almost like a child's pinkie fingertip. Around the Dornoch area cowries are – or certainly were in the seventies – relatively rare. Over the course of three weeks' worth of studious beach-combing we might only find two or three between us.

We would each select a patch of sand and inch our way forward on hands and knees, eyes darting around to pick out the tell-tale perfectly formed little shells, perhaps moving a stone to inspect what lay underneath or brushing a few grains of multi-coloured sand from a tiny mound, only to be disappointed to find a still pretty, but less coveted, smooth and milky-pale pebble, or a little fragment of mother-of-pearl, and always careful to avoid kneeling on any spiky sundried seaweed. Our eyes would only leave the miniature sandy landscape, inches away from our faces, to sneak a look at each other's progress. If one of us was successful we would whoop triumphantly and wave our minute trophy in the air while the other two would have to decide whether to abandon current searches and move to seemingly more fruitful pastures, or keep going doggedly on.

The end of the school holiday would arrive too soon, we would say goodbye to my grandparents, their cats and their house and leave Dornoch and its 'Carlsberg don't do beaches but if they did...' behind for another year.

For any of us children with a new cowrie in our pocket, the sadness of leaving would be tempered with the knowledge of what was to come. Once we'd settled back home, at some point one of us would suggest a game of 'shop'. Due to their rarity, cowries were much prized, and for the price of a cowrie I could buy a week's loan of my sister's favourite ragdoll, several copies of my brother's *Beano*... or pretty much whatever my heart desired.

In 1979 my grandfather died, my grandmother moved to Inverness to be closer to her sisters and holidays in Dornoch stopped. I wouldn't visit again for over 20 years, and when I did many of my childhood haunts were gone, or so changed as to be unrecognisable. The fields beside my grandfather's house had been torn up and built on, the towering rocks we used to leap into the sea from were a shadow of their former monolithic selves, half-buried in the ever-changing sandscape.

The first summer after my grandfather died we spent our holidays on Iona. One morning we decided to walk to the nearby beach. I have a clear recollection of a long straight walk along a road with large flat fields on either side and the constant sound of crickets chirruping. We got to the beach and found a likely-looking spot. One of us must have sat on the sand, picked up a handful of sand to sieve through inquisitive fingers... and found a cowrie. A miracle! Soon we had two excitedly clutched handfuls of cowries each. That beach was forever more in my mind called 'Cowrie Beach'.

Our holiday came to an end and we went home. Each of us was desperate to play shop, to spend the vast riches of cowries that we had accumulated. Perhaps my older sister had a glimmering of understanding but my wee brother and I were at a loss to understand why our cowries, once considered so 'valuable', were now practically worthless.

I sat with a cowrie, dwarfed even in my small hand, my gaze drawn along each line and back and tried to understand what had happened. I still loved my cowries, I could still see that each one was a perfectly beautiful miniature object, but somehow, something had changed.

Last year, on a beach in Cornwall, I found a cowrie completely by chance. I looked around for more, enlisting the help of my three children, but there were none to be found.

The Solsgirth Snake

Leona Skene

The huge metal clasp that held my father's pit bag
    jumble, a mesh string sack, was
A giant's safety pin. Lilliputian, I was fascinated.
    Could never touch,
But stared up goggle-eyed as it lay dormant on the
    kitchen counter.
The orange boiler suit he wore, soot-stained, crumpled
    in a ball
Spoke of Work and Tired and Don't Pester Him.
    I remember
The time he brought a fossil home, glossy, blue-black,
    with the imprint
Of scales, rough, around the outside. It was a snake
    chunk, squat as a sushi roll.
No other thing I had owned had held such dread and
    glamour: such mystery
Ageless, reptilian coal: how I treasured it, clutched it in
    my hand at night
Showed it to other awed six-year-olds, then snatched
    it back.
I have it still. I am older now, and keep it in a drawer:
    it bides its time.

Ma Wee Freen

Ethyl Smith

It's jist a wee white stane, or snow quartz tae be correct,
nae bigger than a fat pea in a pod, and aboot the same
shape. It doesna luk much but it feels amazin when ah
touch it. Thur's nae bumps, nae cracks, jist as smooth as
ye like aifter years o poundin and grindin by the North
Sea. God kens whit size or shape it wis at the stert.

Ah came by it by accident, or maybe it came by me
that first day aifter ah left ma work. Gettin awa for a
day or twa seemed a guid idea, a chance tae try and sort
masel oot. Ah picked ma favourite 'git awa frae it aw'
place and ended up walkin alang the shingle in Pennan
Bay. It wis the month o June, warm and calm, wi a
magic sunset tae feenish it aff, and mak everythin seem
richt wi the world. Straicht aheid wis mile aifter mile o
ripplin watter, aw the way tae the horizon. Ah watched
the waves comin and goin, goin and comin, somehoo
tellin me this wis the first day o the rest o ma life, so jist
git on wi it.

The thocht o this challenge hud me liftin some wee
stanes and skimmin yin aifter anither across the watter.
Ah sorta got intae the rhythm, and each time a stane
wud gang a wee bit further. It wis a guid feelin and ah
kept at it till it wis ower dark tae see whit ah wis dain.
And then, withoot thinkin, ah must hae popped this
parteeclar stane intae ma pocket. Ah dinna mind dain it
but a wee while aifter, when ah wis taen aff ma jaicket,
ma new freen drapped oot, landed at ma feet, and oor
special relationship began.

Ah often sit and amuse masel by runnin the wee,
roond stane in and oot ma fingers lik a worry bead, or a

bit o a rosary. It passes the time withoot ony effort for ah seem tae feel an energy comin frae it, remindin me aboot the connection atween earth and sea, and hoo nature's ahint awthin.

Naebody can see it restin in ma haund. And it's aye there when ah need it, jist lik ma ain wee secret weapon, wi every eventuality covered.

Them as ken aboot stanes say quartz haunds the maist energy on the planet and can gie it oot ony time, ony place, as and when ye need it. Micht be true, for ane time it calms me doon, anither it helps me concentrate, and it aye stops me blurtin oot somethin best left inside ma heid. Lik that time at a posh weddin when ah jist kent the happy couple wur wrang for ane anither. Ah wis fine till the meenister asked, 'Is there any person here who believes these two people should not be joined together.' That's when ah near choked, and wis left grippin ma stane, bitin ma tongue, and forcin masel tae bide stoom. It did come tae pass though. They wurna happy, and did split up. But at least they wur spared yours truly announcin the truth tae the world and spoilin their special day.

And then thur wis ma best freen's funeral. That time ah did want tae speak, tae pay her the compliments she deserved. Ah wisna sure if ah'd manage. But ah did. Ma wee stane atween ma fingers kept me calm, and allooed me tae staun up and say the richt words in the richt way.

Ma wee piece o quartz has helped me mony's a time. Noo ah jist expect it tae happen. Ma only worry is maybe drappin it and no kennin. Supposin onybody else noticed they wudna gie it anither glance. They'd never guess a wee thing lik that maittered, or could dae as mony things. In truth ah'd be lost withoot it, and wud never find anither yin the same.

110

Jewellery

An Rud às Prìseil Dhomhsa

Catriona Lexy Chaimbeul

B' e m' Auntaidh Cairistiona a thug dhomh an rud às
prìseil dhomhsa. 'S e bràiste beag tionna a th' ann a bha
le piuthar mo Sheanair, Seonaid, agus bha e air a
thoirt dhìthse le gaol mòr a cridhe, Sandaidh.

Bha Sandaidh agus Seònaid gu mòr ann an gaol agus
an dùil pòsadh. B' e seòladair a bh' ann a Sandaidh agus
bhiodh e tric aig muir airson miosan. As deidh aon
thuras a bha glè fhada, thill Sandaidh le droch naidheachd.
Bha e falbh le boireannach eile nuair a bha e leis an
deoch agus bha ise a-nis trom le leanabh.

'S na làithean sin, b' e cùis-naire a bh' ann dha
boireannach trom bhi air a fàgail leatha fhèin is mar sin,
ged a gheall Sandaidh gur e mearachd a bh' ann agus
nach robh e idir airson a bhith leis an tè eile, chuir
Seònaid an ìre dha a' dhleasdanas a dhèanamh. Thuirt i
ris falbh is gun tilleadh gu bràth. Rinn Sandaidh mar a
dh' iarr i ach, mas do dh' fhalbh e, thug e dhi bràiste
beag tionna le na facail *Forget me not, Jessie* sgrìobht' air.

Phòs Sandaidh am boireannach eile agus dh' fhuirich
e còmhla rithe gus an do dh' fhàs an leanabh mòr agus,
nuair a bha e cinnteach gun robh e air dèanamh a'
dhleasdanas, dh' fhàg e am boireannach eile agus thìll e
chun bhaile far an robh Seònaid fhathast a' fuireachd.

Cha robh Seònaid air pòsadh no air lorg duine sam
bith eile a thigeadh faisg air Sandaidh ach fhathast cha
bu dùraig dhi mathanas a thoirt dha. Ged a bha e a'
fuireachd sìos a' rathad, cha bhruidhinneadh i ris.
Chaidh na bliadhnachan seachad ann samhchair gus mu
dheireadh, bhàsaich Seònaid.

Bha a corp na laighe san taigh-faire ro latha

a'tiodhlaigeadh gus am biodh cothrom aig muinntir a' bhaile tighinn agus urram a thoirt dhi. Nam measg, bha Sandaidh, na sheasamh luigeach aig an doras. Dh' iarr e air mo Sheanmhair (nighean a piuthar?) Seònaid fhaicinn ach cha leigeadh i dha. Nach b' e esan an duine a mhìll a beatha, a thug air falbh an aon cothrom a bh' aice airson gaol? Ach dh' iarr e agus ghuidh e oirre agus bha e a' coimhead cho brònach 's gun do dh' fhairich mo Sheanmhair truas ris. Leig i e a-steach dhan taigh agus chaidh e gu Seònaid.

Agus le sin, thug Sandaidh a thaing dhan teaghlach agus dh' fhalbh e. Tha mi creids gu do smaoinich e gun robh e dubh dha Seònaid as deidh na rinn e; gun do ghabh e brath oirre a dh' fhàg i searbh gu bràth. Ach nuair a chaidh an teaghlach gus sgioblachadh na beagan gnothaichean a bh' aice, lorg iad am bràiste beag tionna. Bha i air a chumail sàbhailte fad na bliadhnachan a chaidh seachad. Dh' iarr Sandaidh air Seònaid gun dìochuimhneachadh air. Agus cha do dhìochuimhnich.

To read this story in English, please visit http://www.scottishbooktrust.com/reading/treasures/small-tin-brooch.

Celtic Wedding Ring

Des Dillon

Scots steel tempered wi' Irish fire
Is the weapon that I desire.
Hugh MacDiarmıd

With this ring I did wed intimacy
with solitude. Two strands knitting holy
crossings soldered with tears of gold weaving
threads of spirit. I thank my God for you
in this his still and silent place of peace.

But I myself had never come to rest
in Scotland separated by heated
religion and London's tendons blood deep
in landscapes, oil and bleats of lonely sheep.
Yes I marched with Irish swagger hurling
and re-hurling prejudice and abuse
from the high wire of Catholicism
onto the laments of Calvinism:
two parallel strings of separation
singing keyless in this bastard nation.

Now dawn points an unexpected road home
for me. Gaels la Cheile[1], Taigh Ceilidh[2], Cois Tine[3]
winding again together yours and mine.
In this ceilidh house an Irish fire burns
while I lean my brio on my elbow,
hound curled at my feet, the blue ocean
whirling in his hair and foam whispering
to his ears of a fresh spring tide flooding.

With this one truth bright in his eyes
and a fiddle jigging somewhere of course,
being years still before my final bed,
unpredicted and surprising, Scotland,
with this ring, with this heart, with this head
and Gaels together onward; I thee wed.

[1] Gaels together.
[?] Cellidh house.
[3] Irish: by the fireside.

'Return to Happiness'

Christine Ashworth

The locket cradled in my palm is etched with a tiny curve of lily of the valley. I finger the worn gold-plate to prise it gently open and study a faded, sepia photograph of my mother. She is leaning into the camera as though to see me better and looks much younger than I ever remember her, and so carefree. I tilt the trinket in my hand to study my brother opposite her, and see that she has bent forward to put her hands on his shoulders and nestle him against her body – two oval miniatures have been cut from the same print. My brother gazes from under a thick fringe, his neat shirt collar visible below his jumper, and seems older than his age, a mere 18 months. The picture was taken in 1939. My father, Charlie Weir, had signed up to join the 8th Argyll and Sutherland Highlanders, a brigade of the 51st Highland Division, and his company was posted to France. Before he set off, my mother gave him this little keepsake of the family he was leaving behind; he cached it in his pocket.

On the seventh day of June 1940, in an orchard in Picardy, Charlie's company was among the first to suffer mass surrender to the enemy. Soon, almost six thousand British soldiers, mainly from Highland regiments, were being marched through France and Belgium plagued by blistered feet, empty bellies, parched throats and sheer humiliation at capture of the legendary 51st Division.

After being floated down the Rhine on a lice-infested barge, Charlie stepped on to alien soil to experience his first taste of the Third Reich regime. Like the other prisoners, he was crawling with ectoparasites and ordered to strip. Clippers were passed over his head, chest and groin until he was as bald as a newly-shorn sheep.

His thin battledress was returned, laundered, and he checked his pockets. Nothing. The memento of his precious family, about the size of his thumbnail, had been lost in the wash or perhaps, purloined by enemy hands.

Crammed with others in a cattle-truck he was rattled by rail deep into Germany, and on arrival at Stalag 1Xc questioned with chilling efficiency by a thin-lipped, blond officer who tagged him Prisoner of War 3369. Charlie turned to leave the holding area where fellow Argylls – all now officially designated POW – were being interviewed, and was arrested in his tracks by a curt command. 'Wait!' He looked over his shoulder to see his interrogator apparently engrossed in paperwork – and the locket lying on the table, just within reach. 'I think it's yours', a voice snapped, 'take it!'

He pocketed his trinket and fled the room. It was one of the few gestures of decency he was to receive from his captors, but a crucial one. When he lay in his bunk, he would treasure a lingering look at the photos of his wife and son. And their images were shared with his fellow captives. Someone in his quarters would say, 'Can I see your photographs for a minute, Charlie?' When the boys were in danger of losing heart, his bibelot was tangible proof that they had family at home waiting for them.

By spring 1945, Charlie had known prolonged hard labour which included felling trees in the forests of Thuringe, laying roads around the town of Erfurt, and in miserable conditions, toiling 60 feet underground in a salt mine. Now, he and his fellow men were emaciated after eight months of abject hunger due to the cessation of critical Red Cross food parcels. A German guard let slip the reason why – stations had been bombed, German communications were being severed. Charlie felt a glimmer of hope and fondled the locket, striving to imagine what his son might look like, aged seven years.

117

He heard shelling all around the area and suddenly POWs were ordered to abandon camp. Mindful of the locket being confiscated on arrival in Germany, he secured it in his kitbag. On marching eastwards to escape falling bombs, Charlie's squad was ordered abruptly onto the back of a lorry and his gear abandoned by the roadside.

Within the week they met up with American tanks and within one more day, his group was flown to Amersham. Charlie set foot on British soil with only the threadbare uniform he stood in. He barely gave his kitbag another thought because soon he was feasting his eyes on his wife and young son, and had wrapped them in his arms, wishing never to let them go.

It is 1975. On a visit to Loch Ness with Mum, Dad looks up a friend from the prison camp. Although they have not been in contact since their incarceration, Dad succeeds in locating Bill who invites my parents to visit his home and meet his wife. Thirty years melt in an evening and they have a companionable time together. Before they leave, Mum feels something being pressed into her hand. She stares down at a small piece of jewellery engraved with three drooping bells which seem to bob up and down on a curved stem. The silence is broken by Bill's wife. She murmurs, 'That's lily of the valley on your locket – in the Victorian language of flowers it represents "return to happiness"!'

Bill says, 'Our company was shoved on the march too at the war end. We saw a pile of kit dumped beside the road. We knew it was our boys' stuff and checked it over to rescue anything we could. I knew whenever I found it the pendant was yours, Charlie, but I never saw you again. I'm sorry we didn't know where to find you to return it before now.'

118

The locket's homecoming seemed to release within my dad memories of captivity which he could finally share with us, bringing about fragile closure on a significant part of his life spent in parlous privation. The keepsake was loved by my parents and I treasure it.

Granny Special

Alayne Barton

My granny wasn't your traditional sort of granny. She
wasn't cuddly, she didn't knit and she never baked a
scone in her life. Instead, she rode a tricycle, read Irvine
Welsh and drank more sherry than was good for her.
A beauty in her youth, she maintained an interest in her
appearance into old age; a condition she resented greatly.
She had a sharp tongue and often addressed caustic
comments to those around her, particularly her husband,
but also her children, siblings and sometimes complete
strangers in the street. Because she was as deaf as a post
these arch observations were delivered in a stage whisper,
like Kreacher the house elf in *Harry Potter*, easily audible
to anyone with even the slightest vestige of hearing left.
She was unaware of this, of course, but even had she
known, I suspect it wouldn't have cost her sleep.
Bafflingly, people seemed to overlook this aspect of her
personality; my mother, usually at the end of her tether
with her recalcitrant parent, was often told what a lovely
old lady Granny was, and had to agree through gritted
teeth because, after all, blood is thicker than water.

To us children though, who were never on the
receiving end of Granny's wicked words, she was the
best. She read the tea leaves for us, inventing all sorts of
improbable and hilarious future scenarios. There would
always be pennies to spend in the mobile shop when it
came, she kept a jar of plastic bread tags on her mantelpiece to use as casino chips for betting on cards or
dominoes, and in the bottom drawer of my grampa's
retirement bureau there lurked amongst assorted toys
Animal bars and Cadbury's Fudges in abundance.

(The bureau now has pride of place in my own living room, and if I'm ever blessed with grandchildren that drawer will once more be filled with similar goodies.) She was a great one for birthdays, spending days beforehand rummaging about in drawers and cupboards and finally coming up with bizarre collections of objects that became known within the family as 'Granny Specials'. To receive a 'Granny Special' was a nerve-wracking experience; to say they were hit or miss would not be putting it too strongly. And yet their very peculiarity was a joy. Certainly you wouldn't get a lump of yellow amber, an old pottery marmalade jar filled with buttons, or a pouch of sixpences from anyone else.

Which brings me to my treasure. My granny died in 2003, just short of her 90th birthday. She hadn't been ill but had endured the many inconveniences and indignities of ageing for many years. My grampa and most of her siblings and friends had predeceased her and she'd had enough. I didn't attend the funeral, a decision I'll always regret.

Some weeks later, having completed the awful job of clearing the house, my mother came to visit, bearing my inheritance; the last ever 'Granny Special'.

It's an oval box, made of varnished cardboard and painted cream with a duck egg blue trim. On the lid, which lifts right off, two beribboned saltdough geese perform an eternal mating dance. Inside there are several objects: a facsimile map of Callander in 1898, a blue papier-mache bowl decorated with two stripey cats, a bone ring, an ivory and jet domino (double six), an enamelled pendant with a flower decoration and a genuine tinker's clothes peg, probably dating from the early 19th century. I can guess the relevance of some of these things; Granny was brought up in Callander and I had lived near there for several years too. I had made the bowl for her birthday once. The domino is presumably for luck and perhaps I had admired the pendant as a child. But I have no idea of the significance of the ring or the clothes peg. It doesn't matter though; what's important to me is that my granny took the time to put the box together, that she chose each of its objects with me in mind, and that every time I open it I'm a child again, sitting on the floor in her living room, surrounded by the faint whiff of Croft Original, eating chocolate, playing dominoes and wondering what deliciously rude remark she's about to come out with next...

Betrothal

Carroll Johnstone

You're just a dry cube of compressed cardboard an inch
square. Your peeling brick-coloured paper, though brittle
and wrinkled, still impersonates leather. A smooth-
domed lid is opened by pushing a tiny brass pin.
Inside perhaps a hint of dressing table drawer perfume
and 80-odd years of dust. Curiously empty, nothing but
a thumbnail gash on black velvet where your prize once
stood asking the question. The details of your origin are
revealed on the faded silk which lines your lid. In bold
letters: JEWELLER AND SILVERSMITH, R.M. Kippen,
in elegant script at a stylish angle, the address in different
font again, 33 HIGH STREET, ANNAN. A deep,
dignified *clupp* echoes when your lid is closed. All those
details exposed but none of your story.

Young Kit, six foot four, probably cycled six miles
from the village of Eaglesfield into Annan. He must
have struggled up Lan'heids hill with his bicycle clips on.
How many weeks' wages did you cost him? Then he
would have tucked you in his pocket safe from dust and
time and biked home with his great mane of hair
challenging the wind. I'd guess it was around 1929 or
30. The ring held a promise in that breath between wars.

Do you remember your bike ride in the gangly,
blue-eyed village boy's inside pocket? Or bookish Jean
wi' the a'burn hair, first pushing open that shiny brass
pin to lift the inch of lid and place your secret on her
finger? That was when she and Kit were first 'acquent';
before her knuckles were swollen and his 'locks were
like the snaw'.

To be honest I'd forgotten where this small box was.

There's a dry eggshell crackle as I caress its fragile skin. I had a moment of panic when I thought I might have lost it on my travels. But there it sat like a dried peach stone in an old cigar box with strange companions; a tiny tartan penknife and an acorn from St Remy.

Of course it wasn't this small, empty tattered box, that I was bequeathed. It was the precious circle which it held. My granny did not give me her engagement ring. It was competent Aunt Sadie, on her late sister's behalf, who doled out the keepsakes. I also have the wooden chair where Granny sat, her ankles daintily crossed, reading Burns aloud. The chair's worn curved handles are chipped by her rings.

I carried one of those rings, safe in its black velvet groove, across the ocean and buried it in a box on a bookshelf in New Jersey. Once or twice I pushed the brass pin and slipped the thin gold band with the pinhead diamond on and quickly off my finger. One day I came home and my apartment smelled of unwashed men, acrid, musky sweat and a trace of cheap cologne. Their thieving fingers quick as hummingbirds had plucked out your ring but left you; void and gaping. In the weeks that followed I noticed more things missing, things that didn't matter. I knew it was the neighbours. They bragged of their break-in with sleazy winks and moved out within the month.

But I think more of you, a small crumpled empty cube, than I did of your skinny gold ring. For without your brittle rose petal paper, your half-inch hinge and the promise you once contained, I would not be here.

Indian Ocean Links

Peter Lomax

Unfortunately my grandfather passed away when I was five years old leaving just a few hazy memories of summer holidays visiting grandparents in West Wales.

I was born in 1965, a blessed time compared to my grandfather, who had the misfortune to be a young adult in the First World War and still of fighting age in the Second.

My grandfather was brought up as a Royal Marine orphan, so although too young to fight he endured the First World War as a Royal Marine bugler boy. Part of this time was spent aboard a Royal Navy ship in the Indian Ocean and visiting the island of Mauritius which was seen as strategically important to maintaining shipping lines round the horn of Africa.

Whilst on the island he acquired a pair of cufflinks made from Mauritian 20 cents coins dated from 1877 and 1880.

As you may have guessed these cufflinks survived the two World Wars and now form some of the last connections that I have with my grandfather and a personal treasure that always brings back memories of a man I wish I had known better.

In 1990, whilst at university, I met the person who, 10 years later, was to become my wife. Both her parents are from Mauritius. Our wedding ceremony was a three-day Hindu service in Mauritius attended by my mother who was, for the first time, able to see the island described to her so many years ago by her father. The cuffs of the suit I wore for the wedding service were fastened by those cufflinks which had left Mauritius over 80 years previously.

I now look forward to passing on to our five-year-old boy an heirloom from his joint ancestry and hope that they will remain a reminder of my family past, present and future for generations to come.

The Sapphire

Grace Murray

The tale begins in 1940, in far-off Singapore. One of
Grandmother's sons, George, went out to Singapore to
set up the tramway system. I've seen photos of him – a
dignified, portly gentleman with a fob watch and chain.
He must also have been extremely brave, for one day he
averted disaster.

A street urchin threw a firework under the hooves of
one of the tram horses and it bolted, teeth bared and
mane streaming. The car behind it jolted and swayed,
threatening to overturn and tossing the screaming
passengers about like dice in a shaker.

What would have happened at the next crossing
doesn't bear thinking about, but before that, a passer-by
stepped out in front of the careering horse, lunged for
the reins and hauled it to a standstill. It was George.

The traumatised passengers suffered a few broken
bones, but all survived. One of the most effusive in their
thanks was an elderly Mandarin. George expected no
reward, but the next day a procession of the Mandarin's
servants appeared bearing gifts. The Chinese so venerate
their elders that one of the gifts was an exquisite, pale
blue sapphire for George's mother.

He told his parents all about the incident in his next
letter home, but teased Grandmother by not telling her
the nature of her present; she would have to wait and
see at his next furlough.

Before George's next home leave, the Japanese
invaded Singapore and George was interred in Changi.
He managed to conceal the sapphire from the guards,
determined to take it home to his mother when the war
was over. But it was not to be; few older men survived

127

the camps. When George realised he was close to death, he entrusted the sapphire to a friend.

Scotland, 1946. Grandmother was working at the kitchen sink when she saw a vagrant pause, then come on up the farm track. For an instant, her heart stopped – but no, those of her six sons who were coming home from the war had arrived already. She sighed, dried her hands, and went to cut a cheese sandwich for the tramp.

When he knocked at the door, she was appalled at his pallor and emaciation. She was even more surprised when the living skeleton enquired in cultured tones: 'Are you Mrs Balfour – Mrs Grace Charteris Balfour?'

She nodded, mystified, and the 'tramp' withdrew a screw of paper from an inner pocket and laid the sapphire in her hand, saying, 'This is a present from your son, George.'

The home-bound ex-P.O.W. told her the whole story – of how the sapphire had been passed from hand to hand in Changi as each temporary guardian died. Often, he explained, the holder kept it under his tongue during searches by the Japanese guards.

Grandmother gave the stone to my father when he got engaged, to be set in a ring for my mother. Solitaires were not in fashion then, so the young couple had the stone cut into seven smaller ones – much against the advice of the jeweller who said it was a precious and rare gem.

When my mother died, I inherited the ring because my maiden name was Grace Charteris Balfour – just like Grandmother's. I treasure it because of Uncle George's courage in facing up to the bolting horse and because of the integrity of the Changi P.O.W.s who might have exchanged the sapphire for a loaf of bread, but didn't.

I have a little granddaughter, Grace, whose eyes shine when she hears the story of her great-great grandmother's sapphire. When I'm gone, she will treasure it too.

Your all-singing, all-dancing drinking buddy, restaurant critic and personal shopper all rolled into one concise, informative and entertaining bundle

I'd rather watch my own sister dance in one of the nearby nudie bars than drink in here

Quite possibly one of the best pubs at this address

The cocktail menu in this place will soon sort the chavs from the chav-nots

ISBN 1-905705-05-0

KN-824-811

www.itchycity.co.uk   £3.

IS IT A BIRD?
IS IT A PLANE?

No, it's your all-singing,
all-dancing, Itchy magazine.

The launch issue will be crash-landing near you this spring.
Containing all the usual Itchy gubbins to spice up your life,
as well as all the best in up-and-coming bands, comedy,
competitions and freebie vouchers too. Don't say we don't
treat you right. To get your paws on a copy, e-mail us at:
subscriptions@itchymedia.co.uk

Itchy